CLIMBING GHETTO WALLS

Publication Number 904
AMERICAN LECTURE SERIES®

A Publication in

The BANNERSTONE DIVISION *of*
AMERICAN LECTURES IN SOCIAL AND REHABILITATION PSYCHOLOGY

Consulting Editors
JOHN G. CULL, Ph.D.
Director, Regional Counselor Training Program
Department of Rehabilitation Counseling
Virginia Commonwealth University
Fishersville, Virginia

and

RICHARD E. HARDY, Ed.D.
Chairman, Department of Rehabilitation Counseling
Virginia Commonwealth University
Richmond, Virginia

The American Lecture Series in Social and Rehabilitation Psychology offers books which are concerned with man's role in his milieu. Emphasis is placed on how this role can be made more effective in a time of social conflict and a deteriorating physical environment. The books are oriented toward descriptions of what future roles should be and are not concerned exclusively with the delineation and definition of contemporary behavior. Contributors are concerned to a considerable extent with prediction through the use of a functional view of man as opposed to a descriptive, anatomical point of view.

Books in this series are written mainly for the professional practitioner; however, academicians will find them of considerable value in both graduate and undergraduate courses in the helping services.

CLIMBING GHETTO WALLS

DISADVANTAGEMENT, DELINQUENCY
AND REHABILITATION

RICHARD E. HARDY

JOHN G. CULL

CHARLES C THOMAS · PUBLISHER

Springfield · Illinois · U. S. A.

Published and Distributed Throughout the World by
CHARLES C THOMAS · PUBLISHER
Bannerstone House
301–327 East Lawrence Avenue, Springfield, Illinois, U.S.A.

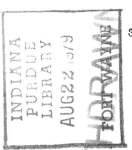

© 1973, by CHARLES C THOMAS · PUBLISHER
ISBN 0–39802865–6
Library of Congress Catalog Card Number: 73–4509

*With THOMAS BOOKS careful attention is given to all details of
manufacturing and design. It is the Publisher's desire to present books
that are satisfactory as to their physical qualities and artistic possibilities
and appropriate for their particular use. THOMAS BOOKS will be true
to those laws of quality that assure a good name and good will.*

Library of Congress Cataloging in Publication Data

Hardy, Richard E
    Climbing ghetto walls.

(American lecture series, publication no. 904. A publication in the Banner-
stone division of American lectures in social and rehabilitation psychology)
    1. Juvenile delinquency—Addresses, essays, lectures. 2. Drugs and youth—
Addresses, essays, lectures. 3. Rehabilitation of juvenile delinquents—Ad-
dresses, essays, lectures. I. Cull, John G., joint author. II. Title.
HV9069.H315   364.36   73–4509
ISBN 0–398–02865–6

Printed in the United States of America
K–8

CONTRIBUTORS

Brad W. Bigelow, Ed.D: Program Director, Nebraska Youth Development Center, Kearney, Nebraska; Consulting Psychologist in Special Education; Licensed Psychologist, State of Nebraska; formerly Chief Psychologist for the Nebraska Penal and Correctional Complex.

John G. Cull, Ph.D.: Director, Regional Counselor Training Program and Professor, Department of Rehabilitation, School of Community Services, Virginia Commonwealth University, Fisherville, Virginia; Adjunct Professor in Psychology and Education, School of General Studies, University of Virginia; Technical Consultant, Rehabilitation Services Administration, U. S. Department of Health, Education and Welfare; Lecturer, Medical Department Affiliate Program, Woodrow Wilson Rehabilitation Center; Consulting Editor, *American Lecture Series in Social and Rehabilitation Psychology*, Charles C Thomas, Publisher. Formerly Rehabilitation Counselor, Texas Commission For The Blind and Texas Rehabilitation Commission; Director, Division of Research and Program Development, Virginia Department of Vocational Rehabilitation. Dr. Cull also has contributed more than fifty publications to the professional literature in psychology and rehabilitation.

Mary L. Dean, M.A.: Counseling Psychologist, Assistant Director, Counseling Center, University of Hartford, West Hartford, Connecticut. Former Director, Project "Teenagers and Law Enforcement"— T.A.L.E.; former teacher and counselor.

Dean Edwards, M.Ed.: Psychologist, Fairfield School for Boys, Lancaster, Ohio. He received his undergraduate degree in Education from Ohio University in 1958 and his master's in 1963 from the same institution. He is presently working on a doctoral program through Ohio State University. Additionally, he has been a psychology instructor since 1965 at the Lancaster Branch of Ohio University. Before coming to Fairfield School for Boys in 1964, he was a teacher in the Ohio public schools for six years.

James O. Finckenauer, Ph.D.: Professor of Criminal Justice and Chairman, Department of Criminal Justice, Trenton State College, Trenton, New Jersey; formerly Assistant Director, State Law Enforcement Planning Agency, Office of the Governor, Trenton, New Jersey; Technical Consultant, Youth Development and Delinquency Prevention Administration, Department of Health, Education and Welfare; formerly a research associate with the Commission to Study the Causes and Prevention of Crime in New Jersey, and Assistant Superintendent of the Ocean Residential Group Center, Forked River, New Jersey; recipient of the New York University Founders' Day Award in 1971; member of Alpha Kappa Delta, National Sociology Honor Society, the American Society of Criminology and the Academy of Criminal Justice Sciences. Dr. Finckenauer currently teaches on the subject of juvenile delinquency at Trenton State College.

Richard E. Hardy, Ed.D.: Chairman, Department of Rehabilitation, School of Community Services, Virginia Commonwealth University, Richmond, Virginia; Technical Consultant, Rehabilitation Services Administration, U. S. Department of Health, Education and Welfare; Consulting Editor, *American Lecture Series in Social and Rehabilitation Psychology,* Charles C Thomas, Publisher; and Associate Editor, *Journal of Voluntary Action Research,* formerly Rehabilitation Counselor in Virginia; Chief Psychologist and Supervisor of Training, South Carolina Department of Vocational Rehabilitation and member South Carolina State Board of Examiners in Psychology; Rehabilitation Advisor, Rehabilitation Services Administration, U. S. Department of Health, Education and Welfare. Dr. Hardy has contributed more than fifty publications to the professional literature in psychology and rehabilitation.

Gilbert L. Ingram, Ph.D.: Coordinator, Mental Health Programs and Chief Psychologist, Federal Correctional Institution, Tallahassee, Florida; Adjunct Lecturer, Department of Psychology, Florida State University; Consultant, Georgia State Department of Family and Children Services, Waycross Regional Youth Development Center; Book Reviewer, *Correctional Psychologist.* Formerly, Chief Psychologist, Robert F. Kennedy Youth Center, Adjunct Assistant Professor, West

Virginia University, Instructor Alderson-Broaddus College, Chief Psychologist, National Training School for Boys, and Research Project Director, Federal Bureau of Prisons. Dr. Ingram also has contributed numerous articles to the professional literature in correctional psychology, crime and delinquency.

J. Wesley Libb, Ph.D.: Director, Ridgecrest Children's Center, Assistant Professor, Department of Psychology, University of Alabama; Consultant, Methodist Children's Home, Selma, Alabama; Consultant, Tuscoba Home for Girls, Tuscaloosa, Alabama. Formerly Psychological Consultant at West Alabama Rehabilitation Center. Dr. Libb has also contributed extensively to the professional literature in clinical and experimental psychology.

Jerry Pollard, M.A.: Psychologist at the Ridgecrest Children's Center, Tuscaloosa, Alabama. Formerly, Statistician, Jefferson County Health Department, Birmingham, Alabama. Formerly, Consultant for State Training School for Girls in Alabama.

Henry Raymaker, Jr., Ph.D.: Chief, Psychology Service, Veterans Administration Center, Dublin, Georgia; Consultant, College Street Hospital, Macon, Georgia; Consultant, Office of Rehabilitation Services, Atlanta, Georgia; Consultant, Regional Youth Development Center, Sandersville, Georgia; Consultant, Department of Family and Children Services, Atlanta, Georgia; private practice, Dublin, Georgia. Dr. Raymaker has been a licensed clinical psychologist in the State of Georgia since 1957 and has his Ph.D. degree in clinical psychology from Vanderbilt University.

Jerome Rosenberg, Ph.D.: Assistant Professor, Department of Psychology/New College, University of Alabama; Consultant, Rehabilitation Research Foundation, Draper Correctional Center, Elmore Alabama; Consultant, Tuscaloosa Association Retarded Children's Opportunity School; Board of Directors, Tuscaloosa Association for Retarded Children, Tuscaloosa Community Crisis Center; Member, Association for the Advancement of Behavior Therapy, American Psychological Association; plus numerous other professional organizations. Formerly, Coordinator of Testing and Evaluation, University Counseling Center, Florida State University. Dr. Rosenberg has conducted numerous workshops in counseling, behavior modification and behavior therapy and is writing in the areas of his professional interest.

Paul L. Rosenberg, M.D.: Resident in psychiatry, Camarillo State Hospital, Camarillo, California; School Consultant, Santa Monica, California. Consultant to the Santa Monica Child Care Centers; Co-Founder of the Los Angeles Free Clinic, Los Angeles, California. Dr. Rosenberg is interested in para-psychology and bio-energetics. He has had extensive experience in the drug abuse field. He resides in Topanga Canyon outside of Los Angeles.

This book is dedicated to

Dr. Charles W. Dean, Director of Institutions
Connecticut Department of Children and Youth Services
and his wife
Mary Lowe Dean, Assistant Director
University Counseling Center
University of Hartford
For their innovative approaches in the treatment of juveniles

The following books have appeared thus far in this Series:

PREFACE

THIS BOOK CONTAINS a blend of descriptive material and practical approaches in working with persons who have been disadvantaged and are delinquent. It is the hope of all contributors that this book will serve as a guide in the process of building a body of tested, practical knowledge in the general area of rehabilitation approaches with delinquent persons.

The book is written for rehabilitation counselors, psychologists, social workers, correctional officers and others who are concerned with problems of delinquency, crime control, and rehabilitation.

A great deal of careful attention was given to the selection of contributors to this book. Appreciation is extended to each of them who worked so hard to develop practitioner-oriented materials devoid of academic cliches and platitudes.

Tactically, the materials are developed and arranged in order to help clarify the thoughts of those in the field and to generate maximum new ideas in order to encourage innovative and positive approaches in rehabilitation.

The chief impetus for the development of this book has been concern about the lack of practitioner-oriented materials for the person on the firing line in the field of juvenile delinquency and crime control.

The perspectives of disadvantagement offered in this book should be unusually helpful in that all contributors are experienced practitioners who understand the effects of poverty, deprivation and their inter-relationships with delinquent behavior.

RICHARD E. HARDY
JOHN G. CULL

CONTENTS

CLIMBING GHETTO WALLS

PART I

Chapter 1

CAUSES OF CRIME
AND DELINQUENCY

RICHARD E. HARDY AND JOHN G. CULL

- RAPID SOCIAL CHANGE
- SELF-UNDERSTANDING AND ADJUSTMENT
- PRISONS AND THEIR CONTRIBUTION TO CRIME
- BIBLIOGRAPHY

THIS IS SURELY a time in American history when concern of most people has reached an all time high over crime, violence, and law and order concepts. Over five million crimes were reported to the police in 1971. This number represented an increase of 11 percent over 1970. Persons in many areas, both rural and urban, are fearful of leaving their homes at night because of violence. It has been estimated that more than 31 billion dollars is the annual economic cost of crime.

Theoreticians and researchers have varied in their explanations of what causes crime. Some have discussed problems within the society and its constantly changing nature and increasing complexity. Others have written concerning chromosomes and genealogy as factors related to crime.

The bias of this chapter will be seen quickly. In the mind of the author there seems to be a definite relationship between poverty and crime (especially those aspects concerning housing, educational opportunity and mental or physical health) and rapid social change and crime. It is not the purpose of this chapter to

5

review and report on the various research projects concerning the causes of crime. The authors simply wish to present some opinions to the reader for the reader's evaluation. This chapter is concerned mainly with the psychosocial aspects of the "normal" offender, and not with abnormality.

Rapid Social Change

Institutions such as the church, the family governmental structures of service, the university and other educational systems, are changing so rapidly that many persons are losing their anchor points for emotional stability. People look around them and find little or no certainty in their jobs, in their family life, or in traditional and religious beliefs formerly held sacrosanct. All of us are deeply influenced by the effects of the mass media such as television. These media to us depict what the outside world seems to have. The outside world seems to have so much more than so many think they have.

Diminishing Value of Work for Work's Sake ("Making It" the Easy Way)

In the early days of the development of this country, the Protestant Ethic played a most important part in bringing about advancements in agriculture, technology and the social services. The amount of hard work which an individual did was a direct indication in many cases of his status in the community. Work for work's sake was highly respected. The Protestant Ethic is now much less an influencing factor on attitudes of persons toward work than it once was. In fact, by the year 2000 it may well be that family attitudes in teaching children such characteristics as dependability and diligence related to work may be drastically modified. Society is moving toward a much greater leisure time involvement. At the present time the effects of this accelerating movement away from the Protestant Ethic are being felt. This means that convincing persons that the way to success is through hard work of an honest nature is becoming even more difficult. Even vocational specialists such as vocational rehabilitation counselors in state and federal agencies are now talking about a movement away from the vocational aspect of rehabilitation services which in itself indicates some drastic changes in the philosophy of many persons in the social service area on vocations and work.

With an increased amount of leisure time and a de-emphasis on full work days or full work weeks, there is more time for all types of activities, including unlawful activities. There seems to be a definite emphasis toward getting what we want the easy way. This emphasis is perpetuated and reinforced by many white collar workers who are able to "get around the law" by various methods. An example is the landlord who puts enough pressure on tenants to receive monthly payments for rent but does not maintain his buildings according to city ordinances. Persons often see different applications of the law applied according to socioeconomic status of the individual accused. Sentences can vary enormously according to whether an individual brings an attorney with him to court, whether the offense is a traffic violation or a more serious one.

Some Characteristics of the Society Which Lead to Crime

We live in a violent society. One which idolizes prize fighters and war heroes. One in which the western robber of the movies is idolized until he is caught—a world in which heroes such as Ian Fleming's James Bond who is "licensed to kill" is respected because he is more violent and gruesome in his treatment of criminals than they are of him and their other victims. Our young military men are taught to kill. The emphasis on violence does not always end with the discretionary thought of the one who is taught to be violent and this fact has been indicated also in the battles of Vietnam when innocent villagers have been killed as well as those who were obviously the enemy.

Americans have necessarily had a somewhat violent and, in addition, fighting spirit. This characteristic has been most important in conquering the wilderness of the west and forging a new nation. Our highly competitive physical effort is constantly depicted in television programs of the wild west. Even the bad man often doesn't seem so bad when he robs or takes what he needs. The so-called bad guy is even respected as long as he is getting away with his activities. The most thrilling scene of a technicolor western is often at the beginning of the movie when the train is robbed and the bandits are able to elude the sheriff and his posse.

Our city areas are particularly vulnerable to violence. A factor which always causes increased social interaction of all types, and crime in particular, is overcrowding. When persons are heavily concentrated in our cities in areas of ugliness, which include poor housing and general discomfort, violent and criminal behavior will occur. When people are concentrated in small areas there are more persons of every type. There are more mentally ill persons including psychotics. There are more physically unhealthy persons, including individuals who are uncomfortable due to injuries which have been ill attended or not attended. Many persons are taking drugs which compound already existing problems and create new ones. Stability is not enhanced by overcrowding. We can expect only a higher incidence of various types of behavior including criminal behavior in that overcrowding in the cities is worsening as our population becomes more urban.

Self-Understanding and Adjustment

Importance of Peer Groups and Role Models

Pressures for conformity come from all sides. Persons in the ghetto feel pressure to conform to the ways of behaving of persons of the ghetto. These behavior pressures are particularly strong among the adolescent groups and especially influencing among adolescent boys. The emphasis seems to be on beating the "system" somehow. This attitude should not be considered an unhealthy emphasis since it represents the wish of most Americans —to somehow get established and find happiness within a social system which is now in constant turmoil and within a society which is in many ways unhealthy.

In order for the person from the ghetto to beat the system, he must either "fake out" some bureaucratic program such as the Department of Public Welfare and get on the public dole, or behave as two different persons. He must demonstrate one type of behavior which will secure his position within his own peer group and demonstrate another type of behavior which will allow him to secure employment in the outside world. His only other alternative is to leave his peer group and those things which he has felt important in order to enter another man's world. It is much easier for all of us to remain in a world which we have known and adjusted to than it is to modify behavior in order to become members of a different society. Think how difficult it would be for most of us to move into a culture different and distinct from our own. The same type of problem and equal in complexity exists for persons who are from impoverished areas, either rural or urban, when they face finding employment and security in the world of work.

Another problem which often leads to crime is that of the lack of sufficient role models for individuals to follow. One of the earliest influences on all persons is that of the parents and much of the early child's play involvement is concerned with the work behavior of adults. When adults within the family are not able to work, children simulate the behavior which they exhibit and this behavior is often characterized by frustration and idleness.

Many individuals who find themselves in trouble need to understand their own motivations or reasons for behavior. The most prevalent reason, for instance, for dismissal from employment is that of inability to get along with fellow workers. Certainly a real cause of crime is inability to get along with persons within the family, on the street, within the community. This is often due to personal immaturity. When there is a basic lack of understanding of human nature—the weaknesses and strengths of all of us—there can be a real tendency to misunderstand that behavior which most of us demonstrate most of the time—self-centeredness. "Rap sessions" held in various community centers may be of substantial value to young persons and older ones too, who wish to come into a group situation in order to discuss problems which they may be having. In addition, they will find support and interest in them as individuals which they may have never found before. Many persons in crime are involved in order to gain attention or recognition, having failed in other areas of life in the highly competitive society of today.

Idleness and hopelessness can be the handmaidens of crime. When persons attempt time and again to find acceptance within their families, but can find no work and no acceptance and must remain idle, crime often results. The hopelessness of many persons is profound, especially in ghetto areas where they must sit on porches or in apartments with inadequate facilities and are unable to join in meaningful activity. Many middle class white collar workers have experienced what might be called "Sunday neuroticism,"—those hours on weekends when he can find little that he may want to do. Many persons are unable to find meaningful activities for themselves outside of their employment. Many are just plainly bored. When employment opportunities are lacking, chances for crime or delinquent behavior are compounded. When employment is found, and is of a menial and meaningless nature to the individual in terms of what he is able to gain from it intellectually, emotionally, or materially, an inadequate adjustment pattern can be established. When the individual has a job which is not commensurate with his capabilities and interests, and the job does not provide what the person needs in terms of materialistic possessions, then the possibilities for crime are again increased. When skills are limited and the work hard and the obvious fact is that most other people have more in terms of material possessions, then the thoughts of delinquent behavior again arise.

All of us are susceptible to our own innate aggression. Some of us are able to control it better than others through sublimation. A highly developed man is able to live and let live without unduly imposing his will or his hurt upon others. Many have not mastered this.

Many people will say that they are not interested in violence and that this innate aggression and tendency toward violence does not apply to them. Certainly it applies to all of us in various ways. Many like prize fighting, some enjoy bull fighting, many are able to vicariously satisfy their violent cravings through hard work, professionalism, or risky activities in sports, etc. Through the ego (will power) we can suppress and in general control or handle our tendency toward violence, especially if we understand our own nature or tendencies to behave in various ways.

Where Crime Occurs

When we look at the areas of the cities in which crime is most prevalent, we find in those areas dilapidated and run-down housing facilities, poor plumbing, unsatisfactory health conditions, both mental and physical, a real lack of the esthetic aspects of life, poor streets, poor garbage collection, poor transportation in and out of the area, few offices of governmental state or federal service agencies, few pharmacies or drug stores, poor schools with some of the most ill-prepared teachers. All these factors and others lead to poor attitudes, poor adjustments, poor mental and physical health and a feeling of inability to escape.

Questions are often raised in rehabilitation service groups concerning how we motivate people. We do not motivate them in our plush offices through counseling and esoteric information when they have to return to poverty or ghetto areas to live. In face, they feel in an unreal world when they are in the office of the counselor and it is difficult for them to respect his judgment when they feel he is not fully aware of their world.

It should be remembered that crime is more prevalent in the areas just described, but also exists in all segments of the society and in all geographic areas. The auto mechanic who steals parts for his automobile from his employer, the highly educated white collar worker who fraudulently files his income tax reports, the businessman who cheats on his expense accounts, and of course, as we know, persons in all strata are involved in drug dependency and abuse. It is important for us to be certain not to brand all persons who live in the ghetto as criminals or prospective criminals. Most people who live in poverty never commit a serious crime.

Prisons and Their Contribution to Crime

The purpose of this chapter is not to outline methods of rehabilitation but to indicate certain causes of crime. Certainly the prison is a training ground in crime. The prison system must be vastly revamped into a rehabilitative and vocationally oriented training program if we are to cut back the high recidivism rate that exists and the high continued crime rate which is prevalent among those who have attended prisons.

Carl Menninger has written a book entitled *The Crime of Punishment*. One of the crimes of punishment is certainly the training which individuals get while in prison—training in being more effective criminals. Imagine yourself a young man who has stolen an automobile and who is imprisoned for several years as a result of a second offense. Your initiation to prison life during your first night consists of your being forced into homosexual behavior by the stronger inmates. This continues far beyond an initiation period and may happen every night when the lights go off in the prison cells. You talk with persons who are third and fourth "timers" who can teach you a great deal about how to be more successful in stealing automobiles and other more expensive items. You get ideas beyond your dreams concerning what possibilities in crime are. There you may meet the leaders in the criminal underworld who will locate jobs for you in crime once you have completed prison training. Violence becomes a way of life. The taking from the weak by the strong is accepted. Those who can defraud others and get away with it are the most highly respected members of this community. The person who can "con" the psychologist or the counselor or the other inmates is also highly respected.

Ramsey Clark in his book *Crime in America* has called prisons factories of crime, and certainly this is an apt description of what takes place within the prison system which is manned in some cases by prison guards with less training and education than the inmates. As long as poorly paid and trained guards and other personnel work in these institutions, we cannot expect for them to be less than training programs in crime. As long as there are large dormitory rooms where many live within prisons where guards do not remain at night there will continue to be mass violence. What has been indicated about prisons also can be said about local jails. Much must be done to improve situations in both.

Carl Menninger has indicated that the use of prisons in punishment only causes more crime. Punishment has actually increased the amount of criminal behavior which the public must bear. There must be massive rehabilitation programs to eliminate these conditions within prisons which are so segregated from the normal community in terms of the basic necessities of life. A very high percentage, approximately 70 percent of those persons who are in the federal prison system, never have a visitor while in prison.

It should be noted that a very high percentage, approximately 25 percent of the prisoners in some state penitentiary systems are mentally retarded. Certainly rehabilitation services, in particular vocational rehabilitation, to those who are physically and mentally impaired can be most helpful.

BIBLIOGRAPHY

Clark, Ramsey: *Crime in America.* New York, Simon & Schuster, 1970.
Menninger, Karl: *The Crime of Punishment.* New York, Viking Press, 1968.

Chapter 2

FAMILIES IN CRISES

GILBERT L. INGRAM *

■ HISTORICAL PERSPECTIVE ON THE FAMILY

■ THE FAMILY AND DELINQUENCY

■ WORKING WITH THE FAMILY IN CRISIS

■ THE FUTURE

■ BIBLIOGRAPHY

THE FAMILY as a viable social unit is under attack from many different sources in modern American society. The assaults have increased in both intensity and number, ranging from criticism concerning the family's lack of effectiveness in producing adaptable members of society, to demands for elimination of the family as it is presently constituted (Cooper, 1970). An immediate result of these assaults is exemplified in the present chapter; many researchers and practitioners are being compelled to look closely at what is happening.

The spectacle is depressing and indeed presents a sad commentary on the family's efficacy as a social unit. Because 50 percent of delinquents come from broken homes, the fact that families are increasingly being broken by desertion and divorce is of

* This chapter represents opinions of the writer and does not represent official policy or attitudes of the Federal Bureau of Prisons or the United States Public Health Service.

immediate concern. Of those units that manage to remain intact, the adult family members manifest their social and emotional problems in various ways, such as alcoholism, drug addiction, crime, and suicide. These problems naturally extend to children of the unhappy families.

Past dissatisfactions of observors toward the family generally were aimed at the lower class of society and thus were more easily dismissed as problems peculiar to that segment of the population. Today, the delinquent products of inadequate, unstable family units are visible in every social class and cannot be so easily ignored.

Theorists and practitioners of diverse persuasions seem to agree that the family is of fundamental importance in the occurrence of delinquency. Every involved discipline, despite differences in emphasis, joins in the general castigation of the family. Typical of these views are the following: It is a truism that for every juvenile delinquent, there is a delinquent home environment. Children are not born delinquent; they are made that way by their families, usually by their parents (CRM's *Developmental Psychology Today* 1971, p. 291). The more thorough a study of juvenile delinquency is, the greater the emphasis laid on the family as a social unit (Pettit, 1970, p. 191).

The family is frequently cited as the villain of many social evils but with regard to delinquency there is almost unanimous agreement. Even in those cases in which other economic, cultural and psychological factors play a major role, the family still remains significant by its failure to counteract these other forces.

Research results notwithstanding, it is possible that this consensus is nothing more than an empty generalization, devoid of any real meaning and worthless for purposes of prevention or treatment. In fact, such a broad indictment of the family may seduce some into thinking that they now understand the problem, when obviously, this is not the case.

Another fallacy in this area is the tendency to use preliminary research results to place a label on a family that seems to breed delinquency. Once this label is available, the assumption is made that a grasp on the cause of delinquency is at hand. Hypostatization is a comforting but nonproductive enterprise. The causes of delinquency are undoubtedly complex and varied, and not unitary.

It is not the intention to present a comprehensive review of all literature pertaining to the effect of the family on delinquent behavior. This task, although necessary, has been accomplished by others, including an excellent review by Peterson and Becker (1965). Rather, the goal is an overview of the area emphasizing general conclusions that appear to have some merit and more importantly, that may have some applicability. Problems in working with the families of delinquents are discussed and specific examples of tactics are presented that may facilitate successful intervention.

HISTORICAL PERSPECTIVE ON THE FAMILY

The modern concept of childhood was unknown in the Middle Ages. At that time, childhood was viewed exclusively as a transition stage before adulthood. As the rate of infant mortality and the demand for productive work decreased, the family began to focus on the child as an individual in his own right. Children were able to go to school and refrain from work. Especially during the 17th and 18th Centuries with the increased opportunity for education, childhood assumed the status of a separate stage of development. Adolescence as a separate stage was even later in evolving, not appearing in its present state until the late 19th and early 20th Centuries.

During most of the 19th Century, the agrarian-based culture predominated with its independent family unity and a cohesive community life. As the industrial culture grew, family structure loosened with the concentration of populations in the large, heterogeneous communities. The shift was not only rural to urban, but also included an increased immigration from Europe to the big cities of this country. It should be noted that separate courts for juveniles were first established in the late 19th Century after the large metropolitan courts were swamped with an increasing number of juvenile offenders.

Long cited as a puzzling and difficult stage, adolescence gained society's concentrated attention after the late 19th Century. Because of the rapid technological advances and the influence of mass media, the present situation provides even more stress for the teenager and the family. As Mead aptly stated, "Parents have been rearing unknown children for an unknown world since about 1946 (Mead, 1972, p. 586)."

Added to the ordinary pains and adaptations that occur in growing up during any historical period, today's teenager is placed in various conflict situations. While being bombarded with provocative stimuli and the sight of hedonistic behaviors of adults, the adolescent is taught to remain economically unproductive and to postpone immediate satisfaction for long range goals. Yet, after a prolonged period of protection and abstinence from 'adult' activities, he is supposed to emerge somehow from this dependent status into adulthood fully capable of behaving in a responsible manner. Added to these contradictory messages, which confuse and frustrate most adolescents, are the other social changes that have altered family life.

The size of the typical family has decreased so that each member is interacting with fewer other members, making individual contributions all the more important. At the same time, shared family activity or 'togetherness' has diminished, and this restricts the number of intrafamilial interactions. This trend sometimes prevents the family's carrying out its prescribed social function. The once biological contribution of the family was that of providing economic and physical safety for the members. Today, society expects the family to serve primarily as a socialization mechanism for the child and to provide satisfaction of psychological needs for all family members.

Leadership of the family has shifted in many ways from a patriarchal type to a more democratic or shared method of decision making. The former role of the father, that of providing explicit authority and fulfilling visible economic duties, allowed the children to model after him. He was quickly accepted as the authority figure. The mother's role was also definite and visible. Changing roles plus the extensive impact of mass media have created a situation in which children are less likely to accept the parents as models of behavior. Riesman (1969) has written of the increasing separatism of teenage culture and the massing in schools of large numbers of young people. The atmosphere engendered by this phenomenon is one of questioning the legitimacy of adult authority. In fact, Riesman believes that the young become 'captives' of each other.

The shift in parental roles also has direct effects on the child when problems occur between the parents. One immediate result is seen in the handling of child custody cases. Until recently, fathers were considered to own all family property, including the children. The mother for all practical purposes had no legal rights to them. Today, an almost automatic preference obtains for the mother over the father in such court decisions.

Another characteristic of modern families is their increased mobility. Many writers describe the family as completely inefficient social units, citing the nomadic nature of their existence and resultant lack of stability. All of these modern trends in the life style of family units have dramatic effects on the children. The smaller size of the family plus the frequent changes in residence creates a lack of personal ties with others. Most modern families work and recreate as separate individuals outside of their home neighborhood. It is no great surprise that children of such families feel alienated, disenchanted, and at odds with the world around them.

Granted that modern families have unique problems and do not seem to be satisfying society's expectations; why though do seemingly privileged teenagers become delinquent, especially in terms of violent acting-out behavior? The attribution of such behavior to lower-class versus middle-class persons had been accepted as a general belief in both lay and professional circles. More recently, Stark and McEvoy (1972) among others have challenged this assumption. Using data compiled by the National Commission on the Causes and Prevention of Violence, they cited statistics supporting the idea that, in fact, the middle class is more prone toward physical assault than the poor. Stark and McEvoy suggested that violence among the poor is more likely to become a police matter because of lack of privacy and little recourse to professional counselors or influential friends.

Keniston (1968) has cited one reason for some of the problems of modern families that offers a different perspective on violence. The adolescent's constant exposure to social upheavals occuring during the past decades has afforded an excellent opportunity for disagreeing with parental values and for perceiving between what parents say and what they do. Keniston acknowledged that there has always been a failure to live up to professed ideals, but heretofore the adolescent has learned when parents can be reasonably expected to practice what they preach. Today, this "institutionalization of hypocrisy" does not occur so easily because rapid social change does not allow for the easy definition of exceptions to the rule and it is much easier for youth to detect such discrepancies. Ironically, the young hold to those values (love of fellow man, equality for all) which their parents espouse but do not practice. Having been raised in an affluent environment, the adolescent feels outrage over the lack of opportunities for those less fortunate. Added to this general feeling of anger and disappointment with his parents is the ever-present fear caused by the threat of the bomb and possible technological death. The awareness of violence is continually reinforced by frequently publicized mob behaviors.

Whether the cause is frustration over living conditions, personal inadequacies, or as Keniston has suggested, an obsession concerning violence in general, there is little doubt that the tendency to act out antisocially is increasing among youth in all social classes.

Today, if the family were considered to be a small business enterprise, it might have to declare bankruptcy. The task of turning out a useful social product is not being accomplished. In a recent large-scale study, the authors concluded that most teenagers do not achieve emotional autonomy, detachment from the family, or a personal ethical code of behavior (Douvan & Adelson, 1966). Although these manifestations of inadequate families are possibly as significant as delinquency, none produce such immediate and tangible damage against society. While the financial cost of delinquency is astronomical by all estimates, the psychological and sociological effects are undoubtedly a greater liability for everyone.

THE FAMILY AND DELINQUENCY

Numerous studies have been conducted in the investigation of family characteristics and delinquent behavior. Too many of these studies suffer from severe methodological weaknesses. The typical strategy used in those studies that seem to satisfy research requirements has been a comparison of families of delinquents with families of non-delinquents. This shotgun approach has been necessary because no systematic theory is available to guide inquiry and to organize existing data. The growing emphasis on differential classification programs and the concomitant development of differential treatment approaches acknowledge what every practitioner knows; i.e., delinquents do not present themselves as a homogeneous group for research or treatment purposes. Similarly, families of delinquents have their own particular 'personality' and do not as a single group share similar characteristics.

Rubenfeld (1967) identified the lack of a framework for family classification as a serious drawback in any attempt to determine the effect of family life on delinquent behavior. However, his suggestion for categorizing families by use of child-rearing patterns, such as those determined by the Fels Institute, may also be a waste of time. For example, after reviewing the enormous amount of data on the effect of different child-rearing practices, McCandless (1967) presented his advice which seems most appropriate:

> . . . . . mothers [parents] who are well-meaning and who try relaxedly to do what they sincerely believe is best for their children—particularly when this is in harmony with the cultural ways of the community with which they are most closely associated—obtain the best results with their children (McCandless, 1967, pgs. 127–128).

We have little reliable data on the subject considering the widely scattered attention directed toward it.

Despite the lack of information concerning the family, research findings have indicated possible characteristics that may bear on the problem. Three general types of families have consistently been identified with delinquent behavior: an unhappy, disrupted home with poor structure; a home in which parental attitudes of rejection prevail, and; homes demonstrating a lack of consistent and adequate discipline. Whenever possible, representative studies from both the earlier and the more current literature are presented.

Disrupted Homes and Delinquency

Families may be disrupted by the physical loss of a member through death, divorce, or separation, or by the lack of structure caused by disturbed or criminalistic parents. Many studies in this area have been devoted to the effect of father absence on delinquent males, but the investigation of that variable has been a recent phenomenon.

A widely held assumption had been that the mother produced the major effect on the children and the father was relatively unimportant. Freud's writings were largely responsible for this focus on the mother's role, and even his critics seemed to agree with him on this one issue. The effect of maternal deprivation dominated the literature for many years. However, as more interest developed concerning the father's role, studies began to demonstrate the influence of the father, particularly concerning delinquency. Glueck and Glueck (1962) cited repeated instances of alcoholism, nonsupport, brutality, and frequent absence from home in the fathers of delinquent boys. Extreme difficulties with male authority figures were frequently noted (see Medinnus, 1965) but disturbed relations with mothers were present only for a few delinquents (Brigham, Rickets, & Johnson, 1967).

As attention was directed more toward the father, new problems were encountered which interfered with research. If the family is intact, fathers usually work during the day and have to be contacted on evenings or weekends. Because this involvement entails the loss of leisure time, fathers are less likely to cooperate. Fathers also view themselves as having little to do with their children's problems because they share the same cultural bias that others have. If the father is unavailable, researchers have frequently adopted another approach which has severe limitations; namely, interviews are held with the mother to obtain information about the father. Distorted perceptions are typically obtained, either positively biased when the home is intact or negatively biased when the home is broken. Both kinds of distortions interfere with comparisons of fatherless homes and intact homes.

Available data from those studies that have been conducted on the effect of fatherless homes indicate that the way in which the father leaves the family is an important variable. For example, loss of either parent through death does not seem to be as harmful an experience as a separation because of parental discord.

When the father is absent from the home, the effect apparently centers on disturbed social behaviors for boys. Father absence produced poor sex typing (Bach, 1946) and poor social relations (Stolz, 1954). Because these factors have been associated with delinquency, the effect of father absence on delinquent behavior seems quite important. The question of the relation of the child's age when father absence occurs to subsequent delinquent behavior is another issue far from being settled. Lynn and Sawrey (1959) and Siegman (1966) found that father absence before age five often produced compensatory masculine behavior in adolescence. More recently, Biller (1971) reviewed the literature and concluded that absence during the elementary school years was most important for the development of delinquency.

The importance of father absence for delinquency is not limited to lower class children. Siegman (1966) asked a group of medical students anonymously to reveal their early histories. Minor behavior problems such as cheating in school were equally likely to occur in both father-absent and father-present groups, but serious acts such as theft of property occurred more frequently in the father-absent group.

Recognizing the importance of a variable and isolating its particular effect are two entirely different problems. Although many studies do support the notion that fatherless homes frequently result in delinquency, approaching the problem simply in terms of father-absence versus intact homes has yielded no definitive answers. Hertzog and Studia (1968) reviewed 59 studies dealing with the effects of fatherlessness on children in general and 13 studies dealing directly with delinquency. They found general support for a relationship between delinquency and father-less homes but also noted qualifying factors. Their suggestions for future research included a shift from single variable analysis to a study of interacting clusters of factors. The fact that approximately six million children in the United States are being raised in fatherless homes indicates the urgency of proceeding with definitive studies.

Contrary to earlier writings, absence of the mother is not frequently cited as a major factor in the area of delinquency. Most researchers apparently agree with Becker, Peterson, Hellmer, Shoemaker, & Quay (1959) who reported the role of the father as being apparently more important than that of the mother in the development of delinquent behavior. More recently, as the role of the mother has shifted in our society, some attention has been directed toward the possible influence of working mothers on children. However, most studies indicate that that type of temporary absence is not a significant factor.

Emotional disturbance on the part of either parent, which also produces a lack of structure in the home, seems to be instrumental in producing disturbed delinquents. Delinquents who are regarded as emotionally disturbed often have disturbed parents (Becker, et. al., 1959, Liverant, 1959, Peterson, Becker, Hellmer, Shoemaker, & Quay, 1959, Richardson & Roebuck, 1965). Many practitioners have discovered that delinquents have character-disordered parents when they attempted unsuccessfully to work with them (Reiner & Kaufman, 1959). The presence of disturbed or criminalistic parents does not distinguish delinquents from other groups, but it does indicate that homes disrupted by disturbed as well as absent parental figures may indeed contribute to antisocial behavior.

Homes also may be disrupted by the lack of physical space and by the chaotic life style that accompanies such an environment. These characteristics typically describe the lower class family, but as already stated, lack of structure is not confined to the physical aspects of the home. In this sense, middle-class children also are often exposed to a living style that precludes a stable pattern of existence. One immediate result of such disrupted home-life for children from all social classes is to make them more vulnerable to the influence of antisocial peer groups (Peterson & Becker, 1965).

The specific ways in which broken and disrupted homes contribute substantially to the delinquency problem are just beginning to be identified. For example, Wood, Wilson, Jessor, and Bogan (1966) found that the overwhelming feelings of powerlessness that delinquents have in dealing with society can be attributed partly to the lack of meaningful structure in their family life. As yet, few research findings in this area have been substantiated and none have been shown to offer meaningful ideas for application in the real world.

Parental Rejection and Delinquency

Rejection of the child by either or both parents has long been cited as one important factor in aggressive behavior by numerous researchers. For instance, Updegraff (1939), in reviewing the literature concerning the influence of parental attitudes upon the child's behavior, found a positive relation between maternal rejection and overt aggression in the child. Similarly, Baldwin, Kalhorn, and Breese (1945), using data from the Fels project, found that rejected children showed a marked tendency toward quarreling, increased resistance toward adults, and sibling hostility. Bandura and Walters (1959) and Andry (1960) found rejection by the father to be a significant pattern for their delinquent samples. McCord, McCord, and Howard (1961) conducted an extensive study involving direct observations of behavior for more than five years. One of their relevant findings was that parents who generally rejected their sons were most likely to produce aggressive boys. More recently, McCord, McCord, and Howard (1963) suggested that antisocial aggression depends more on the degree of rejection and other parental behaviors than simply the absence or presence of parental rejection.

A great deal more has been written about the effect of parental rejection on a particular type of delinquent or criminal, namely the psychopath. This cruel, defiant person who personifies the laymen's stereotype for all delinquents deserves some special attention because he exhibits extreme variations of behavior found in many delinquents.

Lipman (1951) presented a view which may be taken as a general orientation. He said that the psychopathic child is one who has been rejected from the beginning. Subsequent aggression is almost a compulsive act and no feeling for other people is present. Bender (1961) stated that psychopathic behavior occurs when the child is exposed to early and severe emotional and social deprevation attributable either to impersonal institutional care or to critical blocks in the mother-child relationship. Fox (1961) proposed that the psychopath's lack of internalization of cultural values could result from his unfortunate first contact with society, i.e. extreme rejection by the parents.

This has an interesting analogy in research conducted on animals. Harlow (1962) found that monkeys raised in isolation had severe social abnormalities that could be compared to psychopathic behavior. Among other types of behavior, they showed exaggerated aggression and an absence of affectional interaction. This seems to indicate that the influence of early social relationships on aggressive behavior may hold despite species differences.

Psychopathic behavior has been proposed to stem from parent-child relationships other than extreme rejection. Greenacre (1945) reported the fathers of psychopaths to be usually men who spend little time at home and who act in a cold manner toward the child. The mother was not a steady parent in her interactions with the child or with others. Jenkins (1960) proposed, in addition to the possibility of organic involvement, that the child may have been exposed to a confusing situation for social training. All of these proposals are generally in agreement with the research cited above. Despite the post facto nature of the writings, they point to a rejecting environment early in life as a causal factor in aggressive behavior and possibly in the etiology of psychopathy.

Parental Control Techniques and Delinquency

There are three general ways in which parental reactions seem to contribute to delinquency: (1) Parental attempts at discipline are inadequate to control antisocial behavior; (2) Parental reactions provide a punitive model for the child to imitate; and (3) The parents deliberately encourage the child's inappropriate behavior.

The inadequacy of parental discipline in controlling the delinquent's behavior has been noted by many researchers. Healy and Bronner (1926) and Burt (1929) noted that defective parental discipline was an important social determinant of delinquent behavior. Merrill (1947) determined that most of her delinquents came from homes with lax, erratic, or overly strict discipline. Glueck and Glueck (1950) found that the delinquent's parents, particularly the father, had the same difficulty with discipline. Bandura and Walters (1959), Bennett (1960), and McCord, et. al., (1961) cited the inconsistent handling of problem behavior by parents as a factor in delinquency.

The effect of inadequate discipline is hypothesized by Hoffman and Saltzstein (1967) to be the weak development of conscience frequently found in delinquents. Apparently the type of discipline exerted by the parents does not facilitate the increased resistance to temptation which is necessary to prevent antisocial acts.

The second way in which parental control techniques may lead to delinquency is by providing an aggressive model for the child. Bandura, Ross, and Ross (1961, 1963) found that children, especially boys, are influenced by viewing aggressive behavior, and more importantly, become more aggressive themselves in other situations. The significance of these studies is magnified by the fact that parents of delinquents resort more often to aggressive behavior for punishment than do other parents (Glueck & Glueck, 1950, McCord, et. al., 1961).

Physical punishment may effectively suppress behavior for a short period but it frequently causes a great deal of frustration and provides another opportunity for the delinquent to learn to be aggressive. As Sears, Maccoby, and Levin (1957) found in their classic study, the pattern of child-rearing that produces the most aggressive children is when the parents disapprove of aggression but punish its occurrence with their own physical aggression or threats of aggression.

The third, and perhaps most insidious manner by which parents may influence the expression of delinquency, is the deliberate encouragement of antisocial acts. A great deal of data has been collected which supports the hypothesis that delinquent behavior is reinforced by the family. Shaw and McKay (1942) and Glueck and Glueck (1950) both found that their delinquents came from homes in which other criminals were living. McCord and McCord (1958) discovered that a criminal father plus the absence of maternal warmth was the one combination most likely to lead to delinquent behavior. Similarly, dropping out of school, which typically accompanies delinquency, is related to the parents exhibiting the same behavior (Williams, 1963).

The above examples of general reinforcement of delinquency are overshadowed by the occurrences of direct antisocial instruction by the parents. Bandura and Walters (1959) noted that parents of aggressive boys tended to encourage aggression. Bandura (1960) found that mothers of aggressive boys were punitive when aggression was expressed toward them but became more tolerant when the aggression was expressed toward peers or siblings. Becker, Peterson, Luria, Shoemaker, and Hellmer (1962) reported that mothers who frequently used physical punishment also frequently told their children to fight other children whenever necessary.

WORKING WITH THE FAMILY IN CRISIS

Although increasing evidence indicates that families are doing a poor job of rearing children, one conclusion remains inevitable under our present system of justice; the family can not be ignored in either the prevention or treatment of delinquents.

In reviewing the history of the development of juvenile courts in this country, Mennel (1972) concluded:

Today, as then, we can no longer disqualify parents from caring for their children simply because they are poor or unfamiliar with the principles of child psychology. Parents may indeed abuse or fail to exercise their disciplinary authority. There is, however, little histori-

cal evidence to indicate that public authorities in the United States
have provided viable and humane alternatives [Mennel, 1972, p. 78].

Until realistic alternatives are available or society changes its
viewpoints regarding the sacrosanctity of the family, involvement
of the family is necessary. Even after the delinquent's behavior
has become completely unmanageable, the situation in which he
does not have to return to his basic family unit would be the rare
exception. Unfortunately, even in this case or after incarceration
has been effected, the courts have no legal authority to insist upon
the parent's involvement in the treatment of the child.

Experience to date indicates that successfully involving the
family in the prevention or treatment of delinquency often is dependent upon the individual expertise and initiative of the change
agent in overcoming bureaucratic inertia. Few specific suggestions are available from the research literature. However, a full
understanding of many of the problems facing the family in crisis
better prepares the worker to facilitate this involvement. Several
parental reactions to delinquency occur frequently enough to
warrant some attention. These reactions include a denial of blame
with subsequent anger directed toward society, guilt after-the-
fact and a feeling of helplessness, and finally, passivity and a re-
linquishing of responsibility because it is now out of their hands.

The Hostile Family

Many families confronted with the fact of their child's delinquency react very negatively. Typically, these are multi-problem
families for whom delinquency poses an additional crisis. Already
overwhelmed with financial and social misfortunes, the family is
ill-prepared to deal realistically with the child's situation. Most
hostile families fall into society's lower social classes.

Previous interactions between family members and society's
representatives usually have been in relation to problems in the
educational system and frequently have been negative experiences. Against this background, the appearance of another 'helper'
in the life of the family may be greeted with anger and sometimes
overt hostility. Communication often breaks down because of real

differences which exist between the values and language of the worker and the family.

Not only do the disadvantaged have their own particular vocabulary and style of speech but their concerns in life may differ significantly from the middle-class culture (Miller, 1958). Typical middle-class workers, regardless of discipline, probably share common beliefs about human nature (Dole & Nottingham, 1969). Frequently, the workers' beliefs conflict with the family's own values and communication channels break down. For example, the middle-class emphases on frugality and responsibility probably are not shared by disadvantaged families. Similarly, the family may seem unconcerned with long-term plans because their energies are focused on present problems. Confronted with an unwelcome stranger who talks differently and places a high value on the 'wrong' things, family members may directly indicate their disagreement and displeasure. Any helper, finding his well-intentioned overtures to be greeted thusly, can fall into the trap of assuming an authoritative posture and a condescending manner. The interaction undoubtedly will proceed downhill from this point.

What can be done to work with such a family? The answer depends upon the ability of the helper to understand and accept the members for what they are. This means that he must entertain the idea that the family's behaviors and values may be appropriate *for them*. If he can do that, he should aim at the facilitation of the child's adaptation by working with the family. This process entails his gaining acceptance not as a friend but as someone who can help. Learning the language and values of the family are important because it is the rare middle-class person who fully appreciates the social and personal lives of the lower-class individual. Other suggestions that may be of some use include the following:

(1) Any indications of talking down to the family will reinforce their dislike and distrust of the authority person.

(2) Refusing to state opinions or backing down when confronted by the family will be interpreted as a sign of weakness and interfere with rapport.

(3) Avoidance of some relevant issues for the sake of "being nice" will destroy any respect for the person.

(4) Firmness, not coldness, is the preferred approach.
(5) Programs and suggestions should be geared to the real concerns of the family and not for abstract goals.
(6) Giving the family concrete tools to work with is better than speaking in generalities.
(7) Providing the family with tangible services, if at all possible, will facilitate their cooperation.
(8) Do not expect appreciation, at least in the traditional sense, for these efforts.

Most of these suggestions are self-explanatory. Providing concrete suggestions (#6 above) is discussed in the next session. An example of a tangible service (#7 above) may be the worker's serving as a go-between for the family and the school.

After the disadvantaged child has experienced difficulties in school, attempts by either the teacher or the parent to intervene are usually viewed as interference by the other party. An increasingly negative series of communications may convince the family, for example, that the teacher is either not concerned or is discriminating unfairly against the child. Subsequent school difficulties may be excused by the parents in such an atmosphere of distrust. Serving as a go-between in this case, the worker can make a valuable contribution by soliciting information from the school and by sharing helpful family data with the teacher. One result of such activities may be to discover that the child, accidently or deliberately, has reinforced erroneous assumptions on the part of both teacher and parents. Regardless of the specifics, however, all parties benefit from this type of interchange which minimizes the defensive maneuverings of all concerned.

The best intentions will not always guarantee success in working with the family, especially one predisposed to suspicion and hostility toward outsiders. The practitioner may well find that his contributions are either not accepted or are of limited usefulness. This outcome should suggest another immediate alternative which has proven effective in many instances, namely the use of the community volunteer.

Initial reluctance to use volunteers was a natural reaction from professionals who felt that they and only they could understand and deal with delinquents and their families. However, with the failure of traditional therapy approaches and the scarcity of professionals, the use of lay counselors or family workers has gained in popularity. Using volunteers does not remove the responsibility from the worker. Rather, the professional becomes a case manager at a different level; for example, selection, assignment and training of volunteers is essential for the success of a volunteer program. If done correctly, the use of volunteers can be effective even in the most difficult situations. Carkhuff (1971) has described a successful program to train lay counselors indigenous to the inner-city, typically regarded as one of the most resistive areas to reach with any services.

The Inadequate Family

One frequently finds families that want to cooperate but seem incapable of handling their children or at least have difficulty with one particular child. Sometimes the family has reared several children without delinquent histories but another child has run into numerous difficulties. This child may be a special child in that he has been sickly, retarded, brain damaged, left alone for a period because of unavoidable environmental circumstances, or for one reason or another has been afforded special status in the parent's eyes. The inappropriate handling of such a child may lead to delinquency in any social class. Patterson, Cobb, and Ray (1970) found that the types of processes in the family leading to delinquent behavior were present in all socioeconomic levels.

Assuming that the family does want to help their child or that the worker has prepared them for such involvement, the task of the practitioner is to deliver as quickly as possible to the parents techniques for making successful changes in the child's behavior. For reasons both of efficacy and efficiency, behavioral techniques seem to be the treatment of choice. They are the easiest to communicate, easiest to understand, and have been applied successfully with parents in diverse situations. Using the family itself as an agent of social change allows them to assume primary responsibility for the child which enhances feelings of competence and mastery over their environment. Additionally, the techniques are already being used by the parents but typically in an unsystematic fashion. Minuchin, Montalvo, Guerney, Rosman, and Schmer (1967) discovered that the mothers of problem children in slum areas used reinforcement techniques, but inconsistently and inappropriately for the child's deviant behavior.

Some direct results of inappropriate reinforcement techniques on delinquents have been identified. Delinquents in comparison to non-delinquents, are raised in homes where dependency behavior, approval seeking, and verbalizations of dependent behavior are negatively reinforced (Bandura & Walters, 1959, Bender, 1947, McCord & McCord, 1956). The implications of this extinction of dependency behavior for verbal counseling approaches may explain in part the fact that delinquents do not typically profit from conventional therapy. In fact, Mueller (1969) found that client's behaviors with therapists became increasingly similar to behaviors that occurred within the family constellation.

The strategy of retraining parents to act as more effective behavior modifiers has been successfully applied to parents of disturbed children (see Hirsch & Walder, 1969). The basic idea of using parents as the primary change agents is not only more economical and practical, but Patterson, et. al. (1970) cited evidence suggesting that it may have a more permanent effect. Their program, in contrast with other attempts, concentrated on changing multiple classes of deviant child behaviors rather than altering a single behavior. Some of their specific techniques and findings have wider applicability for working with parents than their particular study. Relevant suggestions from their program are summarized below.

(1) Having parents simply read programmed texts on child management techniques is of limited value. [As adjunct material, these books may be helpful: *Child Management,* Smith & Smith, 1966; *Living with Children,* Patterson & Gullion, 1968.]

(2) Telling parents what to do is not as effective as the actual demonstration of recommended procedures.

(3) Training of the parent in the home has the advantage

of the normal setting but it is a costly procedure. Group training methods are more advantageous once the family becomes involved in the process.

(4) Parents are notoriously inaccurate in remembering their children's early behaviors. Dependable information should be obtained through ongoing recording.

(5) Structuring of home visits is necessary to get an adequate observation of the home. Family members often attempt to avoid the 'intruder' by remaining in an inaccessible location such as the bedroom. It may be necessary to specify requirements of who is to be present and where during these visits.

(6) Observing the behavior of the delinquent by himself is less reliable than watching the behavior of all family members for a period of time.

(7) The verbal behavior of parents (everything is fine now; yes, we understand the problem, etc.) should not be accepted at face value without additional evidence of changes in behavior.

(8) Providing concrete examples of how to apply behavior principles to everyday problems is more easily understood by parents than the supplying of textbook answers.

(9) It may be necessary to become a nuisance to the father in order to obtain his cooperation; i.e. contact him daily, have court personnel call him, etc. The worker should keep in mind that the uncooperative father may by unable to carry out his assigned tasks rather than being deliberately resistive.

(10) The parent's starting with a simple behavioral problem between himself and the child maximizes the probability of a successful experience with the techniques.

(11) One goal of family training is to teach the parents to intercede before the child's behavior becomes extreme and before physical measures are necessary to control it.

(12) Parents should be reassured that an improvement in the behavior of one child does not mean that another child

will increase his deviant behavior. Many parents believe this to be true and sometimes are reluctant to initiate change.

The Family of the Incarcerated Delinquent

After delinquency has progressed to the point requiring institutionalization, it is exceedingly difficult to involve the family in rehabilitation of the delinquent. In addition to the predisposing circumstances which may have existed in the family for some time, the incarceration of the child creates additional problems for the family. Many families react very negatively to the institutionalization, preferring to act as if the problem no longer belongs to them. Others use the physical separation as an excuse to justify feelings of rejection that may have originally contributed to the delinquency. Regardless of the underlying factors, it is imperative that staff members attempt to overcome this obstacle to rehabilitation.

Staff time is not sufficient to allow for home visitation, not to mention the expense involved in such activities. Encouraging the family to meet with staff on institutional visiting days has not proven successful. Unless the family is able to afford weekday trips, which would be most unusual, visits mean weekend hours and the resultant absence of key staff members. Moreover, even when all parties are present, family involvement through visits is not regular enough for meaningful interactions to occur. All of these factors add to the communication gaps and lead to misconceptions for both staff and family. The delinquent suffers directly from the lack of family involvement because parental planning is crucial for release programming but more importantly, because the parent's behavior often has been a contributing factor to the delinquent's present situation.

One recent suggestion has been to invite groups of parents of delinquents to the institution for week-long visits (Stollery, 1970). Teams of staff counselors evaluate the delinquent's behavior and plan a unified program for him in conjunction with all family members. This program has the added advantage for low income families of providing a type of family vacation as contrasted with the brief, intermittent visits which may serve as a financial punishment. When groups of parents visit at the same time, it serves to facilitate a sharing of mutual concerns between families. Relaxed communications within the family are stimulated by the structured recreation time and reinforced through the group discussions. Staff as well as family members gain by the family's appreciation for the child's situation, especially pertaining to institutional procedures. Although there are numerous problems inherent in such a program, the results suggest a need for additional innovative attempts along these same lines.

One possible outcome of this type of visitation program may be the family's realization that they are unable to provide the necessary controls for the child. This conclusion is often at odds with their wish for him to remain in the family. After the family accepts their own limitations, they should be much more open to suggestions for new approaches. In this case, for example, a day-care program such as the one described by Post, Hicks, and Monfort (1968) may be appropriate. The child is kept in the home which avoids the guilt or other feelings accompanying removal. However, during the day the child is engaged in a program at a community center which also allows further work with the family. This type of program is less expensive than institutionalization but is more structured than total release to the family setting.

Another possible finding of family evaluation may be that the child cannot be helped by his own family. If the needs of the child can not be met within the natural family, a foster family may serve the purpose. Witherspoon (1966) described the advantages of foster home placements for juvenile delinquents, particularly when removal of the child from the home community is necessary to interrupt the established chain of delinquency. Special training is of course important for the foster parents as well as counseling to prepare the family to relinquish their legal claims to the child.

Both of the above programs provide alternative modes of action which may be necessary in compensating for some family deficiencies.

THE FUTURE

Despite the growing number of attacks on the family, it probably will continue to exist in its present form for some years. Rather than attacking the family with no productive goals in view, society's energies should be invested in researching the family's effects on delinquency and in modifying existing weaknesses with available resources.

Developing typological approaches to delinquency along dimensions other than social class has proven to be a promising research activity. Similarly, identification of types of families that contribute to delinquent behavior in combination with other factors may prove to be productive. Glueck and Glueck (1970) have combined these two ideas in their latest work with their Social Prediction Scale. They identified three types of delinquents and families from which they come: (1) Core type delinquents who have, among other characteristics, inadequate maternal discipline and no family cohesiveness;(2) Intermediate type delinquents who have some family inadequacies but not as many as the core families; and (3)Failures who came from apparently adequate families. This schema definitely is superficial, especially with regard to recent works on typologies by Quay and his associates (Gerard, Quay and Levinson, 1970) and Warren and her colleagues (Warren, 1969). However, it serves as a beginning in a neglected area of research because it does take directly into account the family's influence on delinquency.

Working with the family to effect changes in their behavior has proven to be extremely difficult. Parents seem to be responding to growing criticism of their child-rearing practices by constantly shifting and bending to please the experts or to conform to their child's expressed wishes. Unfortunately, neither society's experts nor their children knows what is best for the family. If nothing else, until answers are available, parents should at least be encouraged to provide a consistent and clear model of what they believe to be appropriate behavior for the child.

BIBLIOGRAPHY

Andry, R. G.: *Delinquency and Parental Pathology*. London, Methuen, 1960.

Bach, G. R.: Father-fantasies and father-typing in father-separated children. *Child Dev, 17*:63–80, 1946.

Baldwin, A. L., Kalhorn, Joan, and Breese, Fay H.: Patterns of parent behavior. *Psychological Monograph,* 58 (No. 3), 1945.

Bandura, A.: Relationship of family patterns to child behavior disorders. Stanford University, Progress Report M-1734, National Institute of Mental Health, 1960.

Bandura, A., Ross, Dorthea and Ross, Sheila: Transmission of aggression through imitation of aggressive models. *J Abnorm Soc Psychol, 63*:575–582, 1961.

Bandura, A., Ross, D. and Ross, Sheila: Imitation of film mediated aggressive models. *J Abnorm Soc Psychol, 66*:3–11, 1963.

Bandura, A. and Walters, R.: *Adolescent Aggression*. New York, Ronald, 1959.

Becker, W. C., Peterson, D. R., Luria, Zella, Shoemaker, D. J., and Hellmer, L. A.: Relations of factors derived from patient-interview ratings to behavior problems of five-year olds. *Child Dev, 33*:509–535, 1962.

Becker, W. C., Peterson, D. R., Hellmer, L. A., Shoemaker, D. J., and Quay, H. C.: Factors in parental behavior and personality as related to problem behavior in children. *J Consult Psychol, 23*:107–110, 1959.

Bender, Lauretta: Psychopathic behavior disorders in children. In R. M. Lindner and R. V. Selinger (Eds.): *Handbook of Correctional Psychology*. New York, Philosophical Library, 1947.

Bender, Lauretta: Psychopathic personality disorders in childhood and adolescence. *Arch Crim Psychodynam, 4*:412–415, 1961.

Bennett, Ivy: *Delinquent and Neurotic Children*. New York, Basic Books, 1960.

Biller, H. B.: *Father, Child and Sex Role*. Lexington, Mass., Health Lexington Books, 1971.

Brigham, J. C., Rickets, J. L., and Johnson, R. C.: Reported maternal and paternal behaviors of solitary and social delinquents. *J Consult Psychol, 31*:420–422, 1967.

Burt, C.: *The Young Delinquents*. New York, Appleton, 1929.

Carkhuff, R. R.: Principles of social action in training for new careers in human services. *J Counsel Psychol, 18*:147–151, 1971.

Communications Research Machines Books: *Developmental Psychology Today*. Del Mar, Calif: 1971.

Cooper, D.: *The Death of the Family*. New York, Pantheon, 1970.

Dole, A. A., and Nottingham, J.: Beliefs about human nature held by counseling, clinical and rehabilitation students. *J Counsel Psychol, 16:* 197–202, 1969.

Douvan, E., and Adelson, J.: *The Adolescent Experience.* New York, Wiley, 1966.

Fox, V.: Psychopathy as viewed by a clinical psychologist. *Arch Crim Psychodynam, 4:*472–479, 1961.

Gerard, R. E., Quay, H. C., and Levinson, R. B.: *Differential treatment: A way to begin.* Washington, D. C., Federal Bureau of Prisons, 1970.

Glueck, S., and Glueck, Eleanor: *Unraveling Juvenile Delinquency.* New York, Commonwealth Fund, 1950.

Glueck, S., and Glueck, Eleanor: *Toward a Typology of Juvenile Offenders: Implications for Therapy and Prevention.* New York, Grune & Stratton, 1970.

Glueck, S., and Glueck, Eleanor: *Family Environment Delinquency.* Boston, Houghton, 1962.

Greenacre, Phyllis: Conscience in the psychopath. *Am J Orthopsychiatry, 15:*495–509, 1945.

Harlow, Harry: The heterosexual affectional system in monkeys. *Am Psychol, 17:*1–9, 1962.

Healy, W. & Bronner, A. L.: *Delinquents and Criminals: Their Making and Unmaking.* New York, MacMillan, 1926.

Hertzog, Elizabeth, and Studia, Cecelia, E.: Fatherless homes: A review of research. *Children,* Sept–Oct, 1968.

Hirsch, I. and Walder, L.: Training mothers in groups as reinforcement therapists for their own children. *Proceedings of the 77th Annual Convention of the American Psychological Association, Washington, D. C.* 561–562, 1969.

Hoffman, M. L. and Saltzstein, H. D.: Parent discipline and the child's moral development. *J Pers Soc Psychol, 5:*45–57, 1967.

Jenkins, R. L.: The psychopathic or antisocial personality. *J Nerv Ment Dis, 131:*318–334, 1960.

Keniston, K.: *Young Radicals.* New York, Harcourt, Brace & World, 1968.

Lipman, H. S.: Psychopathic reactions in children. *Am J Orthopsychiatry, 21:*227–231, 1951.

Liverant, S.: MMPI differences between parents of disturbed and nondisturbed children. *J Consult Psychol, 23:*256–260, 1959.

Lynn, D. B., and Sawrey, W. L.: The effects of father-absence on Norwegian boys and girls. *J Abnorm Soc Psychol, 59:*258–262, 1959.

McCandless, B. R.: *Children: Behavior and Development* (2nd ed.) New York, Holt, Rinehart & Winston, 1967.

McCord, W., and McCord, J.: *Psychopathy and Delinquency.* New York, Grune & Stratton, 1956.

McCord, J. and McCord, W.: The effects of parental role model on criminality. *J Soc Issues, 14:*66–75, 1958.

McCord, W., McCord, Joan, and Howard, A.: Familial correlates of aggression in nondelinquent male children. *J Abnorm Soc Psychol, 62*:79–93, 1961.

McCord, Joan, McCord, W., and Howard, A.: Family interaction as antecedent to the direction of male aggressiveness. *J Abnorm Soc Psychol, 66*:239–242, 1963.

Mead, Margaret: A conversation with Margaret Mead: On the anthropological age. In *Readings in Psychology Today* (2nd ed). Del Mar, Calif., CRM Books, 1972.

Medinnus, G. R.: Delinquents' perceptions of their parents. *J Consult Psychol, 29*:592–593, 1965.

Mennel, R. M.: Origins of the juvenile court: Changing perspectives on the legal rights of juvenile delinquents. *Crime Delinq, 18*:68–78, 1972.

Merrill, Maud A.: *Problems of Child Delinquency.* Boston, Houghton Mifflin, 1947.

Miller, W. B.: Lower class culture as a generating milieu of gang delinquency. *J Soc Issues, 14*:5–19, 1958.

Minuchin, S., Montalvo, B., Guerney, B., Rosman, B., and Schumer, F.: *Families of the Slums.* New York, Basic Books, 1967.

Mueller, W. J.: Patterns of behavior and their reciprocal impact in the family and in psychotherapy. *J Counsel Psychol, 16*:2, Pt. 2, 1969.

Patterson, G. R., Cobb, J. A., and Ray, Roberta S.: A social engineering technology for retraining aggressive boys. Paper present for H. Adams and L. Unikel (Eds.)., Georgia Symposium in Experimental Clinical Psychology, Vol. II., Pergamon Press, 1970.

Patterson, G. R. and Gullion, M. Elizabeth: *Living with Children.* Champaign, Illinois, Research Press, 1968.

Peterson, D. R., and Becker, W. C.: Family interaction and delinquency. In H. C. Quay (Ed.): *Juvenile Delinquency.* New York, D. Van Nostrand, 1965.

Peterson, D. R., Becker, W. C., Hellmer, L. A., Shoemaker, D. J., and Quay, H. C.: Parental attitudes and child adjustment. *Child Dev, 30*: 119–130, 1959.

Pettit, G. A.: *Prisoners of Culture.* New York, Charles Scribner's Sons, 1970.

Post, G. C., Hicks, R. A., and Monfort, M. F.: Day-care program for delinquents: A new treatment approach. *Crime Delinq, 14*:353–359, 1958.

Reiner, Bernice S., and Kaufman, I.: *Character Disorders in Parents of Delinquents.* New York, Family Service Asso. of America, 1959.

Richardson, H., and Roebuck, J. B.: Minnesota Multiphasic Personality Inventory and California Psychological Inventory differences between delinquents and their nondelinquent siblings. *Proceedings of the 73rd Annual Convention of the American Psychological Association,* Washington, D. C. 1965, 255–256.

Riesman, D.: The young are captives of each other. *Psychol Today,* (Oct.) 1969, 28–31, 63–67.

Rubenfeld, S.: *Typological Approaches and Delinquency Control: A Status Report.* Washington, D. C., Department of Health, Education and Welfare, 1967.

Sears, R., Maccoby, E., and Levin, H.: *Patterns of Child Rearing.* Evanston, Ill., Row, Peterson, 1957.

Shaw, C. R. and McKay, H. D.: *Juvenile Delinquency and Urban Areas,* Chicago, Univ. Chicago Press, 1942.

Siegman, A. W.: Father absence during early childhood and anti-social behavior. *J Abnorm Psychol, 71:71–74,* 1966.

Smith, Judith M. and Smith, D. E. P.: *Child Management.* Ann Arbor, Michigan. Ann Arbor Publishers, 1966.

Stark, R., and McEvoy, J., III: Middle-class violence. In *Readings in Psychology Today (2nd ed.).* Del Mar, Calif., CRM Books, 1972.

Stollery, P. L.: Families come to the institution: A 5-day experience in rehabilitation. *Fed Probation, 34:46–53,* 1970.

Stolz, Lois M.: *Father Relations of Warborn Children.* Stanford, Calif., Stanford Univ. Press, 1954.

Updegraff, Ruth: Recent approaches to the study of the preschool child. III Influence of parental attitudes upon child behavior. *J Consult Psychol, 3:34–36,* 1939.

Warren, Marguerite Q.: The case for differential treatment of delinquents. *Ann Am Acad Poli Soc Sci, 381:47–59,* 1969.

Williams, P.: School dropouts. *NEA, 52:10–12,* 1963.

Witherspoon, A. W.: Foster home placements for juvenile delinquents. *Fed Probation, 30:48–52,* 1966.

Wood, B. S., Wilson, G. G., Jessor, R., and Bogan, R. B.: Trouble-shooting behavior in a correctional institution: Relationship to inmates' definition of their situation. *Am J Orthopsychiatry, 36:795–802,* 1966.

Crime is the web and woof of society. It is not an accident—not just an accident. The amount, the character, and the kind of crime are socially conditioned. The good people who set out to remake the criminal, to better the police force, to expedite criminal justice, to reform the prison, begin at the wrong end—and too late. The story starts earlier; it starts within the milieu in which the criminals grow up.

Tannenbaum

Chapter 3

THE JUVENILE DELINQUENT AND HIS ENVIRONMENT

Mary Dean

Introduction

J uvenile Delinquent is a catch-all concept used to describe a wide range of qualitatively different youth. It has many different meanings in different social contexts. This concept includes everything from the "normal" situational delinquent to the

41

psycho-pathological case. To the judge or policeman, the delinquent is one who commits an act defined as delinquent by law
and who is adjudicated as such by an appropriate court although
the law varies from state to state in defining who is delinquent.
To the psychologist and psychiatrist reviewing the delinquent,
he has a problem of a disordered personality development developing from disordered relations between the child and significant
persons in his psychological field. The sociologist puts greatest
emphasis upon social disorganization and conditions of socioeconomic deprivation. To the "average" citizen, the delinquent
may be a delinquent because of his appearance. To the property
owner, the delinquent may be the youngster who doesn't respect
the lawn. To the parent, the delinquent is not a delinquent but
just a mixed up rebellious "kid."

With such diffuse definitions of delinquency, an exact determination of the extent and nature of juvenile delinquency is impossible. However it might be helpful to see what most studies
indicate about that type of delinquent who comes to the attention
of the juvenile courts. It must be recognized that many of these
delinquents were delinquents long before they are brought to
court and that many are never brought to court. The adjudicated
delinquent is more likely to be a boy than a girl. He is generally
14 or 15 years old when referred, although he exhibited behavior
problems considerably earlier. His attitude is hostile, defiant, and
suspicious. He is from the lower social class, is usually retarded
in school work, especially in reading ability, and shows a chronic
history of truancy.

Types of Delinquency

While, technically speaking, a delinquent is one who has been
declared so by a juvenile court, those so adjudicated represent a
relatively small and non-representative sample of the juveniles
who commit delinquent acts. Further, just as there are numerous
types of delinquency, there are different types of delinquents,
each tending to commit certain types of delinquent acts and each
receiving different treatment. Many studies of juvenile delinquents classify delinquents by type. From these studies, it is possible to describe four types of juvenile delinquents.

The *first* of these, the middle-class delinquent, usually is not considered a delinquent since their class standing protects them from the juvenile court adjudication process. While this group accounts only for a minute portion of adjudicated delinquents, it accounts for a large portion of the delinquent acts committed. Middle-class juveniles are implicated in a large amount of hidden and usually less serious lawbreaking, but this is not to say that there are not instances of serious criminal acts on the part of these youths. They seem to be over-represented in juvenile court for offenses such as traffic, liquor, curfew, incorrigibility, vandalism and car theft cases, while their working and lower class counterparts are over-represented for more serious offenses such as robbery, larceny, truancy and loitering.[1] It has become more evident that in many cases middle-class offenses are generally absorbed by the community, e.g. parents and children working it out with each other, except for the most flagrant violations of the law. Middle-class delinquents known to the police tend not to be involved in repetitive, career patterns of misconduct and once brought to the attention of the police are absorbed back into the community without referral to juvenile court. Only serious forms of middle-class delinquency such as auto theft, joyriding and aggressive behavior end up in juvenile court.[2] Recently much attention has been given to middle-class delinquency and a number of theories have been put forth. It is interesting to note that most theories of middle-class delinquency deal only with boys, perhaps since most middle-class delinquency reported is with boys.

Second, the occasional delinquent or one-time offender is usually charged with a minor violation. These delinquents usually participate in group acts of petty theft or vandalism. Researchers who have examined this type of delinquent find that, relative to more serious delinquents, they tend to come from unbroken homes with little family tension and have average grades in school. Several writers have pointed to types of delinquents in many ways analogous to the description of the occasional delin-

[1] Roland J. Chilton, "Middle-Class Delinquency and Specific Offense Analysis," in VAZ, *Middle-Class Juvenile Delinquency*, pp. 91–101.

[2] Don C. Gibbons, *Delinquent Behavior*, Prentice-Hall, Inc., Englewood Cliffs, New Jersey, 1970.

quent. Adolescents in a slum where racketeering or organized gambling flourishes often becomes assimilated into the existing adult criminal subculture, a process which usually involves normal boys from intact homes. These boys may be delinquent in a legal sense but are not considered as such by the norms of the neighborhood. An excellent picture of the occasional delinquent is given by William T. Whyte in "Street Corner Society" (1943). His "corner boys" were well socialized to the society they lived in. Even though they were involved in occasional drug and alcohol use and minor offenses, they were usually non-delinquent.[3]

The *third* type, the habitual gang delinquent, is the one who usually is involved in more serious infractions, is more likely to be sent to juvenile institutions, and most likely to continue in a pattern of semi-professional criminal behavior as an adult. This group has been described as loyal; from poor residential areas; from families that are more often large, broken and with other delinquent members; poor students in school; anti-social; and from large families with lax discipline. They described themselves as smart, excitable, stubborn and not warmhearted. These descriptions fit with Miller's description (1958) on the focal concerns of the lower class, excitement and smartness and toughness. This type of delinquent is further described as a defective superego type who does not internalize the norms of conventional society and who experiences little sense of guilt over his delinquent acts. Rather he accepts the content of and membership in a delinquent peer culture.[4]

The violations of the *fourth* type, the maladjusted delinquent, stem from personality disturbances rather than involvement with a gang or residing in a slum area. This type of delinquent is characterized by high-tension homes, small families, school retardation, and generally are loners. Studies have shown that this type of delinquent suffers early and severe parental rejection. They were also found to have poor peer relationships and to suffer from social isolation. On a self description inventory they describe themselves as "disorderly, nervous, confused and not de-

---

[3] Task Force Report: Juvenile Delinquency and Youth Crime—The President's Commission on Law Enforcement & Administration of Justice; U. S. Printing Office, Washington, D. C., 1967.
[4] Ibid. pp. 203–204.

pendable." This group has been labeled as "neurotic" and with parental repression and lack of warmth in their background. It should be noted that other research done by several subculture writers indicated that there may be a form of delinquent sub-culture analogous to the maladjusted individual delinquent. Cloward and Ohlin identify a "retreatist" or drug-using subcul-ture which they suggest arises when adolescents, out of frustra-tion or lack of opportunity, seek to escape reality.[5]

Not all delinquency is rooted in tangled pathology, discrimi-nation and deprivation of the slum. For at least a portion of the delinquent population, delinquency may be in part an immediate response to an immediate situation. While it may be true that deeper forces may be operating, the youngster may be seizing upon the opportunity of the moment (perhaps illegitimately), the pressures of others, or in response to a situation for which there are no legal or legitimate responses. This may be termed situational delinquency, an example being auto theft—predomi-nantly a teenage crime.[6]

The Delinquent and Family Relations

The family is the most basic institution for developing a child's emotional, intellectual, moral, physical and social poten-tial. It is in the family that the child learns to control his desires and accept societal rules such as the restrictions on the time, place and circumstances where personal needs may be met. Of all the variables which have been shown to be related to delin-quency, family variables such as parental affection and parental discipline are among the most important. For the most part, so-ciologists and anthropologists have focused on social class and delinquent gangs as etiological while psychiatrists and psycholo-gists have focused on family and personality variables. Neither approach by itself is adequate although each may be more rele-vant than the other for the explanation of certain types of de-linquency.

Family patterns vary by social class. Failure to account for

[5] Ibid, p. 204.
[6] Ibid, p. 205.

the interrelatedness of social class, family variables and delinquency has resulted in a considerable amount of confusion. One
reason for this is that studies based upon officially adjudicated
delinquents exaggerate the relationship between class and delinquency because of biases operating in police and court procedures. Nevertheless there are some characteristics of lower class
families which seem to be related to delinquency. Growing up
in a lower class family involves social, economic and occupational
deprivation. This in turn results in lesser attraction for the family
and for the father, given the emphasis that is placed upon the
man's occupational position and earning power. This is related
to a lower concept of personal and family worth.

The parents in a lower class home have limited resources with
which to manipulate rewards and punishments and thus maintain external control over their children, especially in anonymous
urban areas. This is further complicated by a lesser degree of attractiveness of community agencies such as schools and churches,
therefore their lesser ability to maintain external controls. Lower
class families are also characterized by more family disharmony
and instability. There is a greater likelihood of lax or inconsistent
discipline and discipline focused upon the child's actions rather
than intentions stemming in part from the constraining situation
represented by lower class occupations. There is also less affection within the family stemming from pressures imposed upon
the family by the need to adapt to deprived circumstances. All
of these factors lead to a lesser degree of identification with parents and the subsequent internalization of parental norms. These
variables are reflected in the wide range of research that has
demonstrated a relationship between delinquency and broken
homes, ordinal position, family maladjustment, parental discipline and affection or rejection by family.[7] Each of these will be
discussed briefly.

The most consistent pattern observed by the individual who
is working with adjudicated delinquents is the high incidence of
broken homes. This is not easy to determine exactly the relationship as it is next to impossible to determine the extent of delin-

[7] Op. cit., Task Force Report on Juvenile Delinquency and Youth Crime,
p. 195 ff.

quency in the non-adjudicated control group. With the juvenile court operating under the parents patraiae principle, the court is most likely to assume supervision of the child in a case where both parents are not available. Broken homes seem to be more closely related to female delinquency than to male delinquency and to delinquency in younger children than in older children.

Delinquency has also been associated to ordinal position and to family size. Generally, delinquents tend to come from larger families and from intermediates, that is children having both older and younger siblings. One study showed that over fifty percent of the glue sniffers for example came from families with more than eight children, compared to eighteen percent in the control group. Family size is closely related to social class and ethnic background and these must be taken into account.

Family adjustment has been associated with delinquency. Parental and marital happiness and family cohesiveness are closely related to delinquency as the broken home. Perhaps even more important than parental marital relations is the quality of parent-child relationships. Lax and erratic disciplinary techniques, unfair discipline and harsh physical punishment are all associated with delinquents. Most of this research was based on the perceptions of delinquents and, while these may be important, they may not represent actual conditions.

Another aspect of the child-parent relationship often associated with juvenile delinquency is the presence or absence of parental affection. The Gleucks reported that the most important factor seemed to be the father's affection for the boy. The bulk of the evidence seems to support the contention that at least one loving parent, coupled with consistent parental discipline, tends to mitigate delinquency producing forces. Affection seems to be closely related to the child's internalization of parental values. Assuming that these values support conventional behavior, an affectionate parent-child relationship promotes internalization of conventional values and thus insulates a child against delinquent behavior.

There has been more research on the relationship between delinquency and family than the relationship between delinquency and any other class of variables. Much more effort is needed. Most of the family variables associated with delinquency are also associated with social class. The selectivity of the process by which a juvenile becomes classified as delinquent has not been accounted for adequately in this research but strong relationships have been demonstrated.

The Delinquent and School

Since Albert Cohen's classic work was published in 1961, there has been a steadily increasing body of literature on the relationship between delinquent behavior and the school. Generally the literature maintains that success in school is difficult for working and lower class children. At the same time success in school is requisite to occupational rewards which are emphasized and held forth as being available to everyone. School failure characterizes the vast majority of adjudicated delinquents. This condition appears to be the cause of early juvenile institutions stressing educational programs almost exclusively and this was evident in calling them learning, reform, or industrial schools. School failure on the part of delinquents results from conditions which are deeply anchored in prevailing conceptions and organization of the school system. These conditions include emphasis on middle-class values and behaviors which working and lower class youth are not prepared to meet, irrelevant curriculum, hasty and thoughtless labeling, economic and racial segregation, low commitment on the part of the youth and school intolerance for misconduct on the part of selected students.[8] The juvenile delinquent consistently follows a pattern of school difficulty, truancy, and then delinquency. This relationship, like family organization, is complicated by the fact that boys from the lower and working classes are most likely to experience these difficulties.

The Delinquent and the Neighborhood

The delinquent disproportionately is likely to be from a neighborhood that is low on the socioeconomic scale of the community

[8] Op. cit., Task Force Report on Juvenile Delinquency and Youth Crime, p. 259.

and harsh in many ways for those who live there. The child growing up in this neighborhood experiences few of the advantages and comforts which are taken for granted by his suburban counterparts. In these slum neighborhoods population is extremely dense, families are large, parental attention scarce, legitimate recreational opportunities infrequent and criminal opportunities at a maximum. When a juvenile court has to make a decision about whether to release a child, place him on probation, or institutionalize him, the latter form of treatment is far more likely if the child lives under these disadvantageous and unhealthy conditions.

Summary

Juvenile delinquency includes a wide range of behavior which varies so greatly between jurisdictions that a general definition is impossible. Juvenile delinquents are equally as difficult to describe. The adjudicated delinquent however is far less heterogeneous. The selectivity of the juvenile adjudication process is such that the lower classes contribute vastly more than their share. The typical adjudicated delinquent can be described as a 14½-year-old urban male from a broken or disorganized home, who has experienced difficulties in making an adequate adjustment in school and who subsequently has violated laws while in the company of other youth of similar circumstances. Planning programs for prevention or treatment of delinquency requires altering not only the juvenile but also those conditions which made it seem necessary to the court that he be so labeled and treated.

Chapter 4

SOME INDICES OF PREDICTION OF DELINQUENT BEHAVIOR

HENRY RAYMAKER, JR.

- EARLY DELINQUENT MANIFESTATIONS
- NEED FOR PSYCHOLOGICAL EVALUATION
- JUVENILE DELINQUENTS AND PROJECTIVE TECHNIQUES
- NEED TO BE SENSITIVE TO ORGANIC FACTORS
- SELF-CONCEPT AND THE JUVENILE DELINQUENT
- COMMUNITY RESPONSIBILITY

AT A TIME when crime rates are increasing, especially in offenses by young people, a review of signs of juvenile delinquency or indices of prediction, along with a review of the contribution that a practicing psychologist can make, is appropriate.

The detection of early signs of delinquency is most likely to occur in the home and school. The loss of interest in school subjects and conflicts with authority figures in the home and school often proceed some acting-out behavior which finally force society to respond and make an official case of juvenile delinquency.

It is the sensitivity and motivation of the teachers to make referrals to guidance centers and professionals and the willingness of parents to seek help when these early signs are detected that could lead to a reduction and prevention of juvenile delinquency. Also, parents who are sensitive to early manifestations of delinquent behavior can take corrective action.

Early Delinquent Manifestations

Some of these early signs are resentment of authority figures in the home and school and overt conflicts, resentment of overprotection, resentment of limits and discipline, loss of interest in school subjects and obvious underachievements, confusion associated with inconsistent discipline, impulsiveness associated with permissiveness, suggestibility associated with peer group antisocial influences, frustration in the child and a need for compensatory behavior, compulsive stealing associated with poverty, involvement with drugs which usually has emotional and social motivations, etc.

There are many ways a child or adolescent may show tendencies toward delinquency. Also, in each case there are different origins, meaning and a matter of degree. The practicing psychologist, counselor, teacher, parent and society are faced with understanding multiple forms of delinquency and multiple causes that require an individual and clinical approach.

Need for Psychological Evaluation

To understand a youth and his behavior and formulate predictions a psychological evaluation of the intelligence, achievement, personality and feelings of the youth, along with a family and social history, is necessary. This provides the evidence to determine causes and early signs, needs, frustrations, infer predictions, and plan treatment or guidance.

The majority of young people who come to the attention of psychologists and court workers appear to have normal or average intelligence. Determining this dimension of the youth's profile can make our predictions and placement realistic and will maximize success. We do often see in this population under-achievement in school subjects. Evidence that the youth is functioning below his native or potential level, such as observing that his achievement scores are often below his I.Q. and grade placement, can identify problems which when corrected may prevent delinquency. Many delinquents are functioning below their ability level and are behind in their achievement. One great need which exists in our school systems is to reach these children with remedial instruction and the possibility of these resources existing influences our predictive judgment.

In cases where the juvenile delinquent is mentally retarded and this is confirmed by individual intelligence testing, we can often reduce or control delinquency by removing a major source of frustration by placing the child in a special class within the school system for educable mentally retarded children. This reduces the stress and the feelings of rejection that the retarded child shows, which often is the frustration that causes his delinquency or aggression. The success and acceptance that the retarded child feels in a special class may meet the need that will modify the behavior pattern and increase conformity. Consistent discipline, structure, and appropriate school placement appear to be the treatment needs of the delinquent who is mentally retarded and at the appropriate age referral to the vocational rehabilitation agency is needed. The degree that these resources exist in the community is relative to predicting the behavior of the child.

Juvenile Delinquents and Projective Techniques

In the evaluation of the adolescent a sensitive instrument, which provides the psychologist with a sampling of the youth's feelings, attitudes and types of identifications, is the Thematic Apperception Test, or projective technique. The themes and stories which the youth creates on the picture cards in this technique provide meaningful insights into the youth's underlying identifications, feelings and often reveal long felt frustrated needs. Documentation in these areas may identify signs of the degree of the delinquency trend and needs in the youth's personality that are relevant to prediction and management. Experience shows that projecting hostility and aggression is often one of the most frequent themes that a delinquent develops in the stories he creates on this test.

A second frequent theme is the fact that many youths identify with human figures who are depressed and are moody, introspective, or resentful in areas of authority, restrictions, rejections, etc. A third frequent theme is the fact that many youths also project a need to be successful and identify with human figures who are striving for success and recognition. An observation that we frequently see in average or bright adolescents who are in custody because of their delinquency is an admission of faults and acts of delinquency and projecting desires to be a better and more successful person. They try to give the impression that they have learned their lesson and are going to try to do better.

Sometimes these adolescents show abilities at manipulating. Often, however, their comments suggest an awareness of guilt and a need for help. These are content areas where a majority of juvenile delinquents usually project feelings and attitudes on the Thematic Apperception Test and can be one of the most helpful clinical techniques that the practicing psychologist can utilize.

Need To Be Sensitive To Organic Factors

In the battery of tests used by the psychologist are also measurements that can identify organic brain dysfunctioning. In a small minority of these cases some subtle organic deficit may be partially responsible for aggressive or anti-social behavior. In addition to the tests of intelligence and personality, a sensitive instrument in detecting organicity is the Bender Gestalt test where the child has to copy on paper a series of geometric designs. It is important to rule out organic damage or factors and when identified referral to medical consultation and appropriate treatment and planning may control the aggressive behavior of the child. These awarenesses also help the teacher, counselor and parent to better understand and relate to the child. These determinations are relevant to predictive judgments on the course of the child's behavior and adjustment.

Self-Concept and the Juvenile Delinquent

In predicting the behavior of the juvenile delinquent or esti-
mating response to treatment it is useful for the practicing psychologist to determine the self-concept of the youth. The delinquent usually shows inadequate self-confidence or sees himself
in negative ways and overcompensates for these feelings by being openly aggressive and hostile. The delinquent who maintains
a negative self-image may continue to behave accordingly as a
way of expressing hostility. It is the analyses of the origin of these
perceptions and emotions that often are helpful in achieving self-
awareness and insight and permit the delinquent, psychologist,
counselor, and others to take steps to resolve and modify these
behavior patterns.

The practicing psychologist may be able to infer the self-
concept of the youth from the youth's identifications and projections on the Thematic Apperception Test. As a supplement to
this, a practical approach to determining these self-perceptions
is to ask the youth to write a letter about himself indicating how
he sees himself, how he sees his problems and how he feels. Also,
it is useful to have the youth complete a sentence completion
test as many self-concept projections are revealed by this approach.

Therefore, the practicing psychologist's approach to the problem of juvenile delinquency and the study of prognostic signs is
a responsibility to evaluate the intelligence and personality of the
child or adolescent, determine his needs, attitudes, feelings, self-
concept, review the social history, make recommendations, and
be available as a treatment consultant.

It is in the focusing of the recommendations that a sensitivity
to the indices of prediction is important as we strive to reduce delinquent behavior patterns. That is, the psychologist needs to
make recommendations that may reduce the frustration in the
child's life or meet the particular needs in each unique case that
will remove the causes of delinquency. It is necessary that the
community plan resources that can follow through on these recommendations. They usually include a progressive juvenile court,

child guidance clinics, special education classes and consultation with the school system, social agencies such as rehabilitation services, and professional personnel working together in effective communication and coordination.

A psychological evaluation in isolation of the child's environment and continuing influences and resources is an academic exercise. When needs are documented and resources in the community are lacking, then it is the success which we achieve in getting community and social action to develop these resources that will make each community a low predictive or a high predictive environment for success in reducing juvenile delinquency.

In order to formulate or identify signs or indicators which may be used to infer predictions the clinical case method does reveal a pattern or similarities which suggest areas that are relevant in the etiology, treatment, prognoses and prevention of juvenile delinquency. The inferences from this practical experience can offer some indices of prediction. Also, possible warning or early signs in the general preschool and elementary school age population can assist us when parents, teachers and society respond and try correcting problems or meeting frustrated needs before delinquent behavior is manifested or comes to the attention of the court.

Community Responsibility

It is through a mental hygiene and public health principle of prevention that the magnitude of the juvenile delinquency problem in society must eventually be approached. Juvenile court judges are becoming more aware of the significance of meeting needs, arranging for individual and family counseling and treating the emotional dynamics of delinquency. In this corrective and rehabilitative process the involvement of family, school and supportive service agencies working together can increase the prospect of success as more people see the need for treating causes, frustrations and emotions in contrast to simple removal or isolation of the delinquent from society. It is in the area of social change such as the removal of double standards or the inconsistencies in society that additional progress can be made, as often many causes and signs of delinquency are related to poor examples of adults.

A community which is a dynamic society and progressive can cope with problems of juveniles and create a more favorable environment. The worker in this field needs to be involved in social change as behavior is a function of internal and external motivation and influences.

In summary, juvenile delinquency can be reduced by a community sensitive to early signs and indices of prediction of delinquency and can take corrective action. Also, the child who becomes involved in juvenile court action can be evaluated and helped to become a more satisfied and productive person as the sources of his frustrations are removed by planning and counseling.

A forthright approach is for the community to recognize its problems and try to communicate and offer services for this important group of young people, correct its own shortcomings by removing inconsistencies or double standards, provide healthy identifications for youth and provide adequate education, recreation and guidance facilities.

Chapter 5

PROBLEMS OF THE DELINQUENT ADOLESCENT BOY

BRAD W. BIGELOW

- ■ THE FAMILY
- ■ THE SCHOOL
- ■ THE DELINQUENT
- ■ BIBLIOGRAPHY

THE LIFE of a delinquent is a difficult one. It does not involve his simply waking up on his 14th birthday and stating to the world "today's the day I'm going to start getting in trouble." If so, we could legislate against adolescents celebrating the 14th anniversary of their coming into the world and eliminate all kinds of societal concerns.

One of the things that is so commonly overlooked is that the overt act of delinquency or deviant behavior is the culmination of a series of life experiences that predicate social dysfunctioning. There are many signs that begin to appear long before the child reaches the stage where his behavior acts as an abrasive element on those around him. Starting within the framework of the parent-child relationship, it spreads to relationships outside the house involving peers, schools, community, authority and eventually the courts, with much unhappiness and frustration along the way. The delinquent boy has a tougher "go" than his female counterpart, as the manner in which he expresses his dissatisfaction with the world leads to a great deal more retaliation from those around him.

It would be hoped that exploring the special problems of the delinquent boy would serve to keep us more in tune with the ever-increasing problems associated with child care, whether our role is that of parent, educator, counselor, policeman, judge or friend. Whatever form the delinquent boy's aggressive feelings take, the underlying message is "I want to be noticed, appreciated and accepted." Unfortunately, satisfaction of these needs is never really accomplished in a way that leads to a more positive life-adjustment.

THE FAMILY

The belabored parent usually comes in for his share of the blame, especially when child-care agencies are forced to intervene in the child's behalf. Although one can't discount the influences of the delinquent boy's peer culture and environmental surrounds, a great deal of the groundwork is laid in the parent-child relationship. The Gluecks' have been telling us for years that prediction of delinquency can be a fairly simple process if you consider certain variables such as the father's discipline, mother's supervision, the affection of both parents and the co-hesiveness of the family (8). As the variables are eliminated, chances of delinquency are increased.

One of the apparent voids that exists in the life of a boy who is delinquency prone is pronounced supportive and affectional needs that go largely unmet. Berman has indicated that:

If the mother is ineffective, indifferent or cruel, the child sees her as one who rejects his needs and he rsponds to her as the one who hates him. Her own dependency needs may be such that she finds the infant's needs intolerable. This type of mother most often is help-less, confused, disorganized and dependent. She feels there is no one to satisfy her dependency needs and therefore feels unable to care for the needs of her children. The father also poses a serious prob-lem to the child, since he may either ignore the child or belittle him and be harsh or cruel. This father is devoid of or lacking in his capacity to give love or tender interest to the family. The mother often motivates the child to act out her own hostile feelings toward her husband by getting the child to defy or provoke him. This only causes the child to feel further exploited and embittered (1).

There are also indications that parents unconsciously condone the acting out of the child (11). Aggressive fathers beget aggressive sons and can many times sublimate their own frustrated desires for accomplishment and personal recognition through the boy's deviating behavior. There is also the high premium placed upon "manliness" as opposed to "sissiness," where the boy's physical prowess and need to prove his self-sufficiency is continually reinforced. Some fathers need a delinquent son to enhance their own self-esteem by establishing their superiority over someone who is obviously inferior and unable to retaliate. How many times do we hear the delinquent say "I couldn't wait until I got big enough to beat the Hell out of my old man!"

For the delinquent boy from a fatherless home, aggression and preoccupation with physical strength are a way of compensating and establishing a masculine image. Along with it, there is also the problem where the father figure is inadequate, negative or unsuccessful, which Miller describes as a *model for non-identification* (16). Acting out also serves to create the need for punishment to reinforce feelings of guilt and unworthiness.

Further alienation occurs when the delinquent boy denies unsatisfied oral longings (13). What results then is separation and withdrawal from the love object, as well as striking back at that which is perceived as depriving and rejecting through exploitation or taking what he wants through physical force. For the delinquent, relationships with significant persons are often short-lived or inconsistent.

While underprivileged neighborhoods contribute more than their share of children to the juvenile court, many of them come from homes in which the parents are not sufficiently interested to intercede for the child.

While often disregarded, very significant factors in the boy's maladaptive behavior can be growing up in an overly protective, "smothering" emotional climate where assumption of responsibility, expansion of normal social interest, autonomy strivings and freedom in making independent decisions are discouraged. When dependency is encouraged, hostility is increased. Families engendering such dependency unknowingly contribute to the child's inability at coping with interaction and response to environmental stresses. The antithesis of this is the parent who is overly-critical, destructive, punitive and demanding, who succeeds. in destroying the child's self-esteem and sense of personal worth. In both situations one sees the beginning of uncertainty, self-doubt, fear of failure and need to emancipate. What results is apathy, indifference, inactivity, passivity, and the general feeling that "if I don't try I can't fail."

Rules of Rearing Delinquents

1. Begin with infancy to give the child everything he wants. He will then grow up to believe the world owes him a living.
2. When he picks up bad words, laugh at him. He will think he is cute. It will encourage him to think up "cuter" words and phrases that will blow off the top of your head later.
3. Never give him any spiritual training. When he is 21 let him decide for himself what he wants to be. (Don't be surprised if he decides to be "nothing").
4. Avoid the word "wrong." It might develop a guilt complex. A few years later, when he's arrested for stealing a car, he will feel that society is against him and that he is being persecuted.
5. Pick up after him. This means wet towels, books, shoes and clothing. Do everything for him. He will then become experienced in evading responsibility and incapable of finishing any task.
6. Let him see everything, hear everything and read everything smutty he can get his hands on. Make sure the silverware and drinking glasses are sterilized but let his mind feed on garbage.
7. If you have a serious conflict in opinion with your spouse, fight it out in front of the children. It's good for youngsters to view their parents as human beings who express

themselves freely and openly. Later, if you get divorced, they'll know what caused it.

8. Give your children all the spending money they want. After all, one of the reasons you have worked so hard all your life is to make life easier for your children. Why should they have it as rough as you did?

9. Satisfy his every craving for food, drink and comfort. See that his every desire is satisfied. Denial might lead to harmful frustration.

10. Take your child's part against neighbors, teachers and friends. This will prepare you to take his part against the police.

11. When he gets into serious trouble, apologize for yourself by saying, "I can't understand why he turned out like this. We gave him everything."

12. Prepare for a life of grief. You are apt to have it.

—Author Unknown—

THE SCHOOL

"How can you be at ease with a person who is always evaluating you?"

"When at the end of the course, students ask what will be wanted on the exam, the teacher should worry."

"How can a second-grade class have a history of being troublesome?"

"Every teacher should take at least one graduate course a semester, he needs to know the pain of being a student."

"I'd rather be dead than be a teacher"—high school student.

—The Impact Teacher—(21)

The influence of the school on delinquent behavior cannot be overemphasized. The problems that have already emerged prior to his entrance into a formal classroom cannot be left at the front door of the school. Unfortunately, many schools are ill-equipped to handle the deviant child. Teachers lack adequate training and preparation to deal with the responsibilities of motivating, supporting and reinforcing as well as even identifying the child with special needs.

Mental hygienists consider withdrawal, over-control, rigid conformity, and lack of socialization as much more pathological than the more aggressive forms of behavior that typify the delinquent boy's normal life-style. The extremely assaultive person is often a fairly mild-mannered, long-suffering individual who buries his resentments under rigid but brittle controls. Under certain circumstances, he may lash out and release all his aggression in one, often disastrous, act. Afterward he reverts to his usual overcontrolled defenses. Thus he may be more of a menace than the verbally or physically aggressive "chip-on-the-shoulder" type who releases his aggression in small doses (15). Despite this fact, teachers tend to demand the kinds of behavior that are least conducive to personality development. Punishment, criticism, ridicule and ostracism are the typical methods of responding to the boy who acts out or is a non-achiever. Behaviorists indicate that it is a healthier response to resist an order than to accept it.

Historically, we have placed the least experienced teacher in the beginning grades that probably do more to set the tone for future school adjustment than at any other time in the student's academic career. Holt (10) tells us that:

> We adults destroy most of the intellectual and creative capacity of children by the things we do to them or make them do. We destroy this capacity above all by making them afraid of not doing what other people want, of not pleasing, of making mistakes, of failing, of being wrong. Thus, we make them afraid to gamble, afraid to experiment, afraid to try the difficult and the unknown . . . Why are we afraid to say "I don't know? Because we feel stupid, feel others feel we're stupid or less than adequate . . . sometimes it's a relief to make a mistake so that the pressure of success is lifted . . . Children who depend heavily on adult approval may decide that if they cannot have total success, their next best bet is to have total failure . . . There is a great deal of fear in schools. The adjustments children make to their fears are almost wholly bad, destructive of their intelligence and capacity. The frightened learner is a poor learner . . . It is no accident that this boy or girl is afraid. We have made them afraid, consciously, deliberately; in order that we might more easily control their behavior and get them to do whatever we wanted them to do."

Authorities now postulate that the reason boys do not read as well as girls is that, if reading is predominantly taught by women teachers, then it is a "sissy" activity and must be avoided. We are slowly realizing the need for more male teachers at the elementary level for purposes of identification and emulation. Women teachers have a concern for cleanliness, orderliness and mannerliness that rubs a boy the wrong way. Girls tend to get better grades than boys, with a predictable increase in praise. Even the girl with problems has a better chance for success than her male counterpart. To be a girl means that we are always controlled, lady-like, and polite, while boys are encouraged to act out their feelings, not be submissive, and above-all, "act like a man." These are not the kinds of responses designed to endear them to the average woman teacher. The common methods of dealing with the problemed child are suspension, expulsion or denial of privileges, along with countless other ways of making him feel "different."

Early identification of the deviant child is extremely important. Only recently has there emerged the place for elementary counselors who can assist teachers and families in seeking ways to more effectively work with the elementary student. Too often, the family's only contact with the school is when their child has done something wrong. Parents of the delinquent child usually feel inadequate, inferior and defensive in their relationship with school personnel, and many times have experienced many of the same defeats and frustrations in their own previous school experiences. The increased use of para-professionals and teacher aides can free the teacher to make home contacts, enabling them to share the child's successful experiences, solicit their support and better understand the dynamics of the family situation. Many times the teacher is unaware of the child's interests, talents, and away-from-school activities that could be utilized in motivating classroom performance.

The lack of intervention is naturally a contributing factor to future difficulties for the pre-delinquent boy. The following teacher observations of one student's progress through the grades, quite vividly describes how much is seen but how little is done.

> *Kindergarten*—"Sucks his thumb . . . parent's interested . . . average experience."
>
> *2nd grade* —"Sucks his thumb . . . needs praise . . .

found it difficult to adjust to classmates . . . parents now divorced and it has affected David . . . mother cooperates."

5th grade   —"Slow, does little work . . . is immature . . . mother works, she wants boy to do better . . . new stepfather in spring . . . needs to be pushed."

6th grade   —"Very poor student at the first of the year, but has shown some improvement . . . he rarely finishes anything . . . he does not try . . . trying to discipline himself . . . boy likes to visit and show off on occasions . . . needs much extra help . . . requires strict supervision."

7th grade   —"Below-average ability . . . could do better work but lacks self-discipline . . . fairly well-accepted . . . David desires to do well, but he is easily distracted and easily led . . . as the work grows more difficult, unless given strict supervision or pushed to produce, he may fall behind and resort to mischief or trouble-making to get recognition."

8th grade   —"Craves recognition . . . has been quite a troublemaker at times . . . suspended for smoking on the school grounds . . . mother apparently is ready to give up . . . boy resents stepfather . . . easily led . . . David has been in almost continual trouble this year . . . average work, but lacks the discipline to study regularly . . . he still lies, but does not seem to know the difference between right and wrong."

9th grade   —"Absent too much to evaluate . . . definite discipline problem."

10th grade   —"Not enrolled . . . recently committed to Boys' Training School."

Results of a questionnaire administered to students admitted to the Nebraska Youth Development Center over a three year period indicates that entrance into junior high is apparently the time when major problems begin to emerge. When asked "In what grade did you first experience problems in terms of behavior, achievement or attendance," 22 percent identified the seventh grade. The percentage breakdown is as follows: 1st Grade—6 percent; 2nd Grade—8 percent; 3rd Grade—6 percent; 4th Grade —4 percent; 5th Grade—8 percent; 6th Grade—12 percent; 7th Grade—22 percent; 8th Grade—15 percent; 9th Grade—15 percent and 10th Grade—4 percent.

Authorities suggest (19) that the student, upon entering junior high, is forced to make a rather sizeable adjustment in terms of greater competition, increased performance demands and social responsibilities, reduced personal contact with teachers, as well as continuing need for self-discipline. There are additional problems in terms of choices in curriculum, greater variety of teachers and teaching standards, and a greater need for self-starting and self-direction, which the delinquent boy especially, finds overwhelming.

The majority of delinquent youth coming into institutional settings are more equipped and essentially, quite talented in academic areas that are "doing" oriented (crafts, art, music, woodworking, metalworking, mechanics, etc). It is not surprising that people having the greatest impact upon them are school personnel from the non-academically related areas. It would appear that greater flexibility must be provided in establishing a curriculum for the student that does not fit into the standard performance mold.

THE DELINQUENT

It is necessary to distinguish between the delinquent boy whose battle with himself and others is an individual one and the youthful offender whose thoughts and behavior are directed more significantly by sociological influences (9). The former poses greater problems in change or modification, while the latter composes a large majority of adolescents depicted as "delinquent." Several delinquency self-report studies (18) have suggested that, while participation in minor acts of delinquency is very wide-spread, involvement in frequent and serious delinquent acts is concentrated among youth from families and neighborhoods with many other social problems as well. Life is a series of interactive processes involving people and experiences that have special significance or meaning. While the family definitely contributes to the delinquent boy's attitudes and self-concept, environment then serves as the battleground on which the boy's struggle for an identity is either won or lost. How the environment responds to the delinquent is a very important part of his developmental processes.

There is much discussion on effective child rearing practices. Some authorities feel that controls are an essential ingredient in preventing future maladaptive behavior while others are inclined toward a more permissive and tolerant attitude, to minimize internal psychopathology. Symonds (22) found that the children of dominating parents were better socialized, more orderly, prompt, reliable, sensitive, self-conscious, submissive, shy, retiring and seclusive and had greater difficulty in self-expression than the children from submissive parental backgrounds. Children of submissive parents tended to be careless, irresponsible, disobedient, disorderly, to have difficulties in school and work, and to be forward and self-expressive.

Delinquents from lower-class families often times have, as the basis for their hostility toward society, parents expressing their bitterness, criticism and hatred of the larger society with which they struggle (18). The parents also struggle with agencies such as the schools and the courts—both of which are perceived as being controlled by the upper-class. What we may tend to interpret as overprotection and making excuses for their son's behavior, may simply be an expression of their own lifelong feelings of being suppressed and continually beaten down.

Where the delinquent lives is usually far more crucial than whether a youth comes from a broken home, or whether his family is poor or socially deprived (4). A project reported by the University of Chicago showed that teachers who hold negative stereotypes of low-income youth, particularly about their educability, tend to approach them with hostility (20). One sees the emergence of a cyclical pattern in which one negatively reinforces the other.

It is not unreasonable to assume that solidified family relationships would provide the boy with ways of combatting peer group pressures toward nonconformity and antisocial behavior. This seems to be one thing that sets the delinquent apart from the nondelinquent. If he has been able to remain somewhat psychologically intact because of positive family relationships, subsequent group involvements would tend to be more situational rather than chronic and prone to die a natural death as new interests developed.

Group delinquency represents a struggle for adjustment (4). In such a group, delinquent practices of these youngsters serve their immediate personal and social needs in the same way as approved forms of conduct serve the children residing in the more conventional community areas (12). In the delinquent group, prestige and pride are derived from antisocial acts, from long records of delinquency and from time spent in correctional institutions rather than from conforming to the standards of conventional society. In the delinquent group, aggressive drives can be expressed within the group, both through rivalry and competition, and externally, through the group attitude toward authority (2). Delinquent behavior represents conformity to the expectations of the delinquent group, just as socially acceptable behavior represents conformity to the expectations of the normal group (12).

All adolescents need to feel that they belong, and the delinquent probably more than anyone else. He is deeply immersed in a restless search for excitement. The approved style of life is an adventurous one, filled with exploits that are valued for the stimulation they provide. Much of their vulnerability to delinquency can be based upon what kind of feelings they have about themselves. There is some rather tangible evidence (6) that a good self-concept, undoubtedly a product of favorable socialization, veers slum boys away from delinquency, while a poor self-concept, a product of unfavorable socialization, gives the boy no resistance to deviancy, delinquent companions, or delinquent sub-culture.

We know that if an individual is alientated from society, his self-concept may not include those values prevailing in the larger society. Thus, alienation can produce a deviant self-concept, which may generate delinquent behavior, which in turn may reinforce the deviant self-concept (5).

The typical delinquent dislikes himself, especially in regard to his behavior, his moral self and his family self. He suffers from inner tension and discomfort. He is also too unstable and immature to withstand stress and frustration. Seeing himself as bad and worthless, he acts accordingly. He has an uncertain picture of himself, and is easily influenced by external suggestions and by his environment. He often lacks the psychological defenses necessary for normal self-esteem. The self-concepts of delinquents are much more negative, uncertain, variable, conflicted, and passive than those of nondelinquents. Repeated criminal behavior reinforces and further lowers the already deviant and negative self-concept of the delinquent. He sees himself as "bad" and acts accordingly. This, plus negative feedback from others, confirms and worsens his negative self-concept (5).

Previously, there has been some discussion about the importance of early identification in children who may be delinquency prone. Studies have shown (14) that a number of the child's problems peak at about the age of five, with another high point beginning at about the age of ten and stretching over to eleven. The former age is allied with beginning school while the latter is the age when they begin to worry about the change to junior high school. The height of intense involvements with parents occurs at the age of five, and ten to eleven is the age when children begin to feel the impact of the growth spurt leading to adolescence (17). Even at this stage in their development, we can see emerging resentments and fears, anxiety and depression, destructiveness and anger, submissiveness and remoteness. Such are the portent of future disturbances that affect the child's ability to cope and relate. The first step toward recognizing potential disturbance is to face the reality of the child's feelings in situations of frustration, deprivation, pain, danger or loss. We find it difficult to recognize emotional disturbance because we live in a culture in which, from the early months of life, people are taught to suppress their feelings (17).

Delinquents tend to be active, impulsive, aggressive and rebellious. They search for excitement, have a need to elevate their status, have little interest in long-term goals, and want to be controlled in spite of voiced feelings to the contrary. They tend to feel different from others and, in many cases, they are. Data from various youth detention facilities would substantiate the disproportionate number of youthful offenders with speech defects, problems in auditory or visual perception, impaired intellectual functioning and defective socialization skills, poor coordination, faulty judgment and reasoning, and a myriad of other physical, personality and academic limitations that set them apart from the rest. Their problems are more intensified and acute. They are bombarded with negative reinforcements and lack the emotional, social or intellectual resources to cope effectively. Their life experiences are rejecting and non-supportive. Relationships with others are hampered by suspicion and mistrust, with anticipation of the eventual indifference, rejection or abandonment that have typified their involvement with previous love objects. They have little tolerance for frustration, are easily defeated, and are overpowered when required to think independently. Praise is inconsistent with their self-appraisal while punishment re-enforces feelings they already have about themselves. They are the product of an environment that has little tolerance for the deviant for the one who can't conform or perform and for the one who is defective.

We have generally reacted to the delinquent in terms of exclusion, disapproval, rejection or punishment, rather than acceptance, empathy or support. It is common knowledge that punishment is less effective in weakening a response than reward is in strengthening it. Punishment promotes a negative attitude, frequently arouses counter-aggression, lowers self-concept, leads to fear and anxiety, and can create guilt feelings, which in turn increases a need for punishment. It is easier to punish than reward, reject than accept, or criticize rather than understand.

The alternatives normally considered for the delinquent boy include detention or confinement. Many children held in jail do not need to be locked up anywhere (7). They are unnecessarily confined for many reasons, including the use of jail for punishment or "treatment," poor court policies in relation to the detention of children picked up for delinquent behavior, and the lack of open shelter care facilities for children who need temporary care but not secure custody.

In 1967, the Childrens' Bureau obtained data on the specific offenses of 9,177 jailed children (3). Less than four percent were "offenses against person," such as assault or robbery. On the other hand, slightly over 41 percent consisted of acts that would not have been violations of law if committed by an adult—running away from home, truancy, curfew violations, possession or drinking of alcoholic beverages, and "ungovernability." The low figure on offenses against persons indicates that very few of the children who were held in jail could be considered "dangerous."

The problems of the delinquent boy suggest the need for early identification, intervention, and suitable alternatives to detention or confinement, such as increased use of foster placements and group homes. Schools should be better staffed and willing to accept the responsibility of implementing programs for children with special needs, thus combatting the problems of the "force-out" rather than the "drop-out." The use of volunteer probationers and "Big Brothers" should be expanded for purposes of establishing meaningful relationships with adults in the community. Mental health programs can assist in providing supportive family services to facilitate the parent-child interactive process. And above all, communities can look for ways of making the delinquent a part of it's culture rather than keeping him apart.

BIBLIOGRAPHY

1. Berman, Sidney: Antisocial character disorder: Its etiology and relationship to delinquency. *Am J Orthopsychiatry, 29:* 612–621, 1959.
2. Cohen, A. K.: *Juvenile Delinquency and the Social Structure.* Doctoral Dissertation, Howard University Library, 1950–51.
3. *Corrections in the United States: A Survey for the President's Commission on Law Enforcement and Administration of Justice, Crime and Delinquency,* January, 1967.
4. *Delinquency Today, A Guide For Community Action,* U. S. Department of Health, Education, and Welfare, Social and Rehabilitation Service, 1969.
5. *Delinquents Don't Like Themselves—That's Partly Why They're De-*

linquent, Research Utilization Branch, Division of Research and Demonstration Grants, Office of Research, Demonstration, and Training, Social and Rehabilitation Service, Department of Health, Education, and Welfare, Washington, D. C., March 1, 1970.

6. Dinitz, S., Scarpitti, Frank R., Reckless, Walter C.: Delinquency vulnerability: A cross group and longitudinal analyses. *Am Sociol Rev, 27:* 515–517, 1962.

7. Downey, John J.: *Why Children Are in Jail (And How To Keep Them Out).* U. S. Department of Health, Education, and Welfare, Social and Rehabilitation Service, 1970.

8. Glueck, S., and Glueck, E. T.: *Predicting Delinquency and Crime.* Cambridge, Mass., Harvard Univ Pr, 1959.

9. Hirschberg, J., and Noshpitz, J.: Comments on sociopsychological aspects of juvenile delinquency. *Am J Dis Child, 89:* 361–67, 1955.

10. Holt, John: *How Children Fail.* New York, Dell, 1964.

11. Johnson, A. M.: *Sanctions for Superego Lacunae of Adolescents,* Searchlights on Delinquency. New York, Intl Univs Pr, 1949.

12. *Juvenile Delinquency,* Chicago Area Project and the Sociology Department of the Institute for Juvenile Research, Monograph, Chicago, Illinois, 1953.

13. Kaplan, M., Ryan, J., Nathan, E., Bairos, M.: The control of acting-out in the psychotherapy of delinquents. *Am J Psychiatry, 113:* 1108–14, 1957.

14. Macfarlane, L., and Houzik, M.: *A Developmental Study of the Behavior Problems of Normal Children Between Twenty-One Months and Fourteen Years,* Berkley, Cal, Univ of Cal Pr, 1954.

15. Megargee, E. I., and Mendelsohn, G. A.: A cross validation of twelve MMPI indices of hostility and control. *J Abnorm Soc Psychol, 1962:* 431–438, 1965.

16. Miller, Walter B.: Implications of Lower Class Culture for Social Work. *The Social Service Review, XXXIII,* No. 3, (Sept., 1959).

17. Murphy, Lois B.: Problems in recognizing emotional disturbance in children. *Child Welfare,* December, 1963.

18. Ohlin, Lloyd E.: *A Situational Approach to Delinquency Prevention.* U. S. Department of Health, Education and Welfare, Social and Rehabilitation Service, 1970.

19. Phillips, E. Lakin, Wiener, Daniel N., Harring, Norris G.: *Discipline, Achievement and Mental Health.* Englewood Cliffs, N. J., Prentice-Hall Inc, 1960.

20. *Project Innovation: Seeking New Answers to the Prevention and Control of Juvenile Delinquency,* U. S. Department of Health, Education, and Welfare, Welfare Administration.

21. Reno, Raymond H.: *The Impact Teacher.* St. Paul, Minnesota, 3M Educational Press, 1967.

22. Symonds, P. M.: *The Psychology of Parent-Child Relationships.* New York, Appleton-Century, 1939.

Chapter 6

PROBLEMS OF THE DELINQUENT ADOLESCENT GIRL

J. Wesley Libb
and
Jerry Pollard

MANY YOUNG PEOPLE engage in behaviors upon which society frowns. Such behavior seems a necessary part of the maturational process. We may safely assume that in many ways the delinquent adolescent female is very little different from other girls of her age. Behavior which has earned her the label "delinquent" is frequently the behavior for which the adolescent of middle class or influential family background receives at most a reprimand, if, in fact brought to the attention of juvenile authorities.

Adolescence has been defined as a period of psychological and emotional growth, as a social process whose central aim is to develop a clear and stable self-identification. It is a time of behavioral variation, of testing and trying out different roles. Without this testing of roles we would likely live in a borish world of rigid adults who persist in living the unexamined life and who never change. The adolescent is unique in her variations on the theme of independence, creativity, and in finding out what the world is all about from an experimental standpoint. While adult warnings, verbal admonitions and clarification of long-term consequences of behavior may aid the adolescent in avoiding the cold, hard facts of reality, she most frequently must experience the consequences in her own life space by "doing her own thing." Adult values are critically examined and challenged, and contrary to the thinking of many, largely accepted. Society can profit from the freshness of perspective which our young people bring if we do not react angrily or with alarmed anxiety to the challenge!

We live in an age of affluence, of immediate gratification of needs and of material things given to children as a substitute for emotional support and genuine caring. Our society has stressed freedom of expression and action. This emphasis on liberty when carried to its extreme, may lead to a rejection of authority, especially in those situations where adolescents see laws freely broken by parents and peers. The adolescent often dreams of what will be. She may be convinced that she is entitled to all the material trappings of success she sees everywhere and that she can get it with a minimum of effort—the world owes her a living.

In this chapter we define the juvenile delinquent as any child or adolescent who has been referred to an agency appropriate to such a referral, in most cases the Juvenile Court, and found to have committed an anti-social act as defined by law. Keep in mind that such misdemeanors can refer to any thing from running away from home, sexual promiscuity, theft, and perhaps even murder. In understanding such young people it is beneficial to remember one's own childhood experiences and those of childhood playmates. Few of us would be free of criminal records if we had been accountable for all our deeds.

The delinquent may be differentiated from the non-delinquent adolescent on the basis of the frequency or number and the intensity or severity of delinquent acts and on the basis of the intrusion of corrective learning experiences into the life experience of the adolescent which facilitate the development of alternative socially acceptable ways to handle normal feelings and problems of adolescence.

The term adolescence is frequently defined culturally; i.e., in reference to the society in which the girl lives, as well as developmentally; i.e. in reference to age and physical and psychological development. Usually the years from 10 to 18 are referred to as adolescence. This is the period of life when there are many physical, cognitive, emotional, and social developmental changes. The problems unique to delinquent adolescent girls can best be understood against the background of these normal developmental changes and the conflicts and problems which they introduce.

Research has demonstrated that learning plays a critical role in the development of all behaviors including delinquent behaviors. Consequences of behaviors have been shown to play a most vital role in behavioral acquisition. Delinquent behaviors may serve the function of enabling the adolescent to escape or avoid an intolerably unpleasant situation or of gaining a more immediately rewarding experience. Such behaviors may be symptomatic of the adolescent's inability to delay reinforcement and to work for long-term goals. A frequent problem is that the delinquent adolescent has not experienced some of the major rewarding contingencies that maintain the more acceptable behavioral patterns of mature, well-adjusted adults and most adolescents. Seemingly aversive consequences may maintain behavior because the adolescent is rewarded by the fact that someone notices that she is around only when she misbehaves.

Most authorities feel that female delinquency follows different patterns than male. Girls' acts of delinquency are far more limited in scope and variety than boys. The adolescent female's wayward behavior is restrictd to stealing of the kleptomanic type, to vagrancy, to provocative behavior in public, and to frank sexual waywardness. These offenses are shared by boys, but constitute only a fraction of their repertoire. The primary delinquent act for girls is sexual acting out.

Church and Stone (1968) classify adolescent delinquency into five types on the basis of the psychological origins: (1) normal or casual delinquent behavior, (2) subcultural, (3) neurotic, (4) acting out, and (5) psychopathic delinquency. They state that female delinquency, including sexual delinquency, is likely to be of the neurotic, or the acting-out type. Sexual delinquency may have nonsexual origins, it may be an expression of adolescent revolt. It is often associated with simplemindedness and a passive inclination to do what other people say.

There are other problems in particular to females. Our society is remiss in having few places for a child to go when she is being mistreated at home. It is only after she has come to the attention of the law that provisions are made to meet her basic needs.

Of major concern with this particular group of young people is that the normal developmental changes and problems do not occur in a normal or typical home environment, peer subculture, and/or school background. The importance of an intact family unit is often evident when understanding the special stresses and strains upon delinquent adolescent girls.

Some girls are beaten or sexually molested at home. They may be neglected and left to fend for themselves most of the day and/or night. If they do not have close friends from differing home environments they may not know that this behavior is atypical for parents, and accept even incest as a matter-of-fact occurrence. When matters become too difficult to tolerate, they run. A runaway girl soon finds that there is available an easy way to get food and shelter by prostituting herself. If she does not submit willingly and is raped, she is usually hesitant to go to the police for fear they will return her to her home, or place her in an institution. Many girls in our state institutions have run away from impossible situations and one must wonder if running away was not the only adaptive reaction available in the girls behavioral repertoire. The case of Janet S. is illustrative.

Janet is 15, a well-developed and seductive blond with a cherubic face. Her parents separated when she was a few months old, and before she was a year old her mother married her present stepfather. She does not know her real father—she was told that he cared nothing for her and left. Her mother and stepfather had two girls, and finally a much wanted boy. Janet felt like an outsider in her own family, left out, and that as a stepchild she had to wait on everybody else. The girls had often been told that the parents wished they were boys. The stepfather treated them as if they were boys. In addition, discipline was physical, with whippings and verbal abuse applied liberally. When the younger brother arrived, the parents treated him preferentially. They gave him special presents at Christmas, and they would leave the three girls with their grandparents and take the boy away with them on Friday and Saturday nights. Janet stated that she hated the boy, and wished he would die. Unfortunately, he had leukemia, and died when he was only four. Janet, aged nine at the time, was left with feelings of guilt.

A poor student, with low average or borderline IQ, she received no success experiences at school, and learned early that the only way to get attention was by acting out or becoming sick. She copied the aggressive mannerisms she saw at home, threatening to beat up anyone who got in her way. An attractive girl, she soon found that by skipping school and spending the afternoons in the company of boys, riding around and drinking beer, she got all the attention she craved. The more her peers encouraged her, the more outrageous her behavior became. Her friends were primarily delinquent and at one time or another, had run away from home. They told her that it was a great life —you could do anything you wanted.

Janet says that she was very curious to see what it was like to be on "your own"—that all her friends had run away, and she wanted to. One night after a whipping from her stepfather, she ran. She was 13, and soon found that to get food and shelter she had to allow sexual intercourse. She claimed to have been raped, but realized before she ran the chances that she was taking. When she was returned home by the police, she had to testify to rape charges in court. Her stepfather's people wouldn't speak to her, they looked down on her. She had the reputation of being bad. Her stepfather had drunk excessively since before the marriage. Now there were constant fights between her mother and stepfather and his relatives blamed everything on Janet. She felt that no one cared what happened to her—and said that she didn't care what happened to her or to anybody else, either. She didn't care what people thought, and after her initial sexual experience, she just "kept doing it." She has tried speed, but prefers pot. She is now in a State Training School.

In a way Janet has been successful. Her continued acting out has won her continued attention from her family and approval from her peers. She is "tough." Now they visit her laden down with gifts. They tearfully tell her that they will give her anything that she wants, just "please, please don't run away again." She did run during the first month, then came back and hid behind a tree, crying. She asked to be put in a detention cell, so that she could not run. She occasionally implores outside authority to restrain her, and it is only by this constant testing that she knows anybody cares. She is aware of her, as she says, "tempting impulses"—she is aware that what she wants to do will only get her in further difficulty, but she is unable to control her need for immediate gratification. Delinquent behavior is the only thing that has worked for her.

Some girls are born to people who really did not want to become parents. The children are mistakes, or at best, concomitants of living together. Frequently, such children are either beaten or neglected, and soon learn to fend for themselves. Joyce was such a girl.

Joyce is the oldest of three girls. Both parents had a limited education and both worked. The father was an alcoholic and often in jail. While he was absent his wife would entertain men in the house, and the children repeatedly saw their mother get in bed with someone. They were sent outside to stay until the small hours of the morning. Eventually the parents were charged with neglect, and the children taken by the court and placed in a foster home when Joyce was five. Their totally undisciplined behavior and frequent cursing made them intolerable to the foster parents, and they were placed in an orphanage. The mother saw them once. Joyce stayed at the orphanage until she was 15, then ran away. She went to a metropolis in another state and lived a hippie-like existence in an apartment with three other girls. One girl prostituted, the others would beg pennies in the park. They began smoking marijuana, and soon were "dealing." Their apartment was the scene of many parties, and Joyce tried a wide variety of drugs including hallucinogens. She tried anything that was offered to her, and finally had to be taken to the hospital with an overdose. She does not even know what she took.

She now lives in a group home where her salty language and free behavior have earned her the reputation of a "bad" girl. She wants desperately to be liked, but cannot understand why people react the way they do to her. She has learned no appropriate ways of interacting with adults. Her blustering talk is a defense against the deep hurts she has known. One of her sisters exhibits the same behavior as her promiscuous mother, but Joyce is determined not to wind up the same way. She is having to learn appropriate ways of interacting all over again. She does seem to have some insight into her behavior. When asked why girls run away or take drugs, she answered, "They're troubled children. They're worried. My parents never fussed at me. They never cared."

The following paragraphs discuss normal developmental changes and problems, and attempt to relate to each of these major areas the special concerns of delinquent girls. Physical growth and development play an important part during the early adolescent period. Puberty represents the beginning of reproductive sexual maturity. During this period psychological and biochemical changes make reproduction possible. It is noteworthy that menstruation occurs earlier in girls in the United States than in past years with menstrual 9 and 10 year olds a frequent occurrence. Sexuality begins long before puberty; however, with the onset of puberty and the possibility of pregnancy, the adolescent's thoughts and feelings about sex become more intense. While physical changes are a cause for concern for all adolescents, there are individual differences in how different young people react to these changes. Such differences are largely influenced by how others react to the adolescent experiencing such changes, that is, parental and peer reactions.

Parents who are proud of and comfortable with their daughter's maturation obviously differentially effect the girl's self-perception and expression of her sexuality than parents who are anxious about or threatened by sexual maturation. For many delinquent girls such as Janet the choice of sexual acting out as an expression of sexuality may be reinforced or encouraged by a mother whose own sexuality was stifled, repressed and not permitted healthy expression, or by a mother who takes pride in her own sexual seductivity. Frequently, as in the case of Joyce, the promiscuous adolescent has not had acceptable models available in her life experience. Female models may have been promiscuous or may have been overly restrictive. Overly restrictive models may be totally rejected by the adolescent female. Either predicament may lead to sexual acting out. The girl may feel no worth apart from what she can offer sexually. Interactions with insecure male parent figures who encourage seductivity can support this feeling.

The following two cases illustrate different directions taken by girls with similar problems.

Mary is a tall slim girl of 16. Her long dark hair is always slightly disheveled, and a Mona Lisa smile is usually on her lips. She rarely talks, but her hands are seldom at ease—they twiddle, fidget, and occasionally her fists clench, or her nails dig into her hands. She is the eldest of five children. Neither parent finished high school, and both work. Her father gets drunk on his days off and creates a disturbance in the family. He tells Mary that her behavior is responsible for his drinking. The mother is a weak woman, unable to stand up to her tyrannical husband. She has great difficulty expressing affection of any sort.

Mary doesn't do well in school. She wasn't allowed to go anywhere and had no social life outside her home, no friends, no extra-curricular activities. When she was 12 she dated a man for the first time, he took her to her home, and her father asked him to stay. He stayed for two years. Finally, Mary's father told her to ask him to leave as he was giving the family a bad name. When she was 14, she left home with a boy and another couple, returning after a week when she found that the police were looking for her.

Mary is sexually promiscuous. When she was 11 or 12 one of her fathers drunken friends raped her. She said the word must have gotten around fast, because then all his friends used her sexually. Her father tried to, but she fought him off. When asked why she could say "no" to her father and not to his friends because she said they wouldn't have understood and she just couldn't say "no" to someone she didn't know. This pattern was repeated with the boys she dated. Sex was not enjoyable to her, but she felt it was expected. She feels no sense of worth—she is an object to be used.

Mary knows only one way to interact with males. She has written suggestive notes to men in the office where she worked. She is immature and childlike and terribly confused. She is totally unable to express her feelings in appropriate ways. She blames herself for anything that goes wrong, and expresses hostility by digging her fingernails into the back of her hand, or biting herself. She married as soon as she became 16, because she felt that she had no viable alternatives. She refused to go back home, and did not want to go to a state training school.

Elaine had a similar background, but other learning experiences. She is a stolid girl of 15 with above average intelligence. She is big-boned and would be fat were it not for her solid musculature. Tanned and slow moving, she seems to be overly calm and placid. Her family is a troubled one. Her sister, a year older, just had an illegitimate child. Her younger brothers are truant. Her father has had two years of college and has a steady job. He is depressed and anxious, tending to violent temper tantrums—throwing chairs, beating his head or fists against a wall, or breaking out a window with his fists. Her mother is calm and easy going, cowed by the ill temper of her husband. She, too, attended college.

When Elaine reached the age of puberty her father began to take an intense interest in all of her activities. He read her mail, inspected her room at strange times, and expected her to tell him everything she did. He wanted to see her each night in her bed clothes, pulled up her nightgown "as a joke," felt her body and insisted that she kiss him good night. Elaine was alarmed by these sexual advances and would often cry herself to sleep.

When she was 14 she ran away from home. She was picked up at a boy friend's apartment in another state and placed on probation. She was released to the custody of the family, and the court has worked extensively with them. She kept telling her probation officer that she wanted to leave the family. Finally she was caught skipping school, and was removed from the custody of her family, which was what she wanted. She states that she loves her mother, but is afraid of her father. She takes pride in her virginity, but she states that she is really afraid of what will happen to her sexually. She occasionally takes drugs as an escape, as do a majority of delinquent adolescent girls familiar to the authors.

Elaine cannot tolerate any display of anger. She bottles up her feelings until she explodes in a semihysterical outburst. She has terminated two relationships with boys because of their temper. She is far more disturbed than her outward appearance suggests, but she has intellectual controls, and has learned appropriate ways of dealing with the world. She has not learned to say "yes" to be secure. Perhaps the example of her older, promiscuous sister was sufficient to provide an example of what doesn't work.

Research indicates that unwed pregnant adolescent girls tend to have been rejected by family, peers, and friends. This has frequently led to rebelliousness and immaturity in terms of acceptance of society's standard for behavior. Such girls may feel inferior intellectually, socially, or in physical attractiveness. Self-esteem and sense of identity are seriously marred and the girl is cut off from social learning experiences that foster healthy growth and development.

According to the foremost authorities on cognitive development the typical adolescent develops the ability to reason in hypothetical ways. That is, she learns to think in terms of how situations might be rather than what they are in the here and now. Prior to ages 11 or 12, children have difficulty seeing things in ways other than they actually exist in their experience. Because adolescents have developed linguistic and mathematical symbolic structures, they can use these symbolic systems to represent in fantasy what the situation might be or what might happen if one does this or that. The possible outcome of one certain behavior can be compared to the outcomes of alternative behaviors. These skills are learned. Schools, family experiences, and peer associations promote their development. One consequence of the development of these abilities is that the adolescent can articulate his unhappiness with parents and society as it presently exists and can see alternatives or differences in the way things might be. Such awareness and abilities to express may lead to open conflicts with authority figures where the younger child may show no visible evidence of difficulties. Often the child who later becomes a delinquent has been coerced into obedience or has been permitted to sulk in disobedience. Suppressive, environmental parental controls are generally no longer effective with the adolescent who can now think and develop alternative approaches to the resolution of their feelings and needs. Diana is an illustrative case familiar to the others.

Diana is an obese, sloppy girl of 15. Her parents were divorced when she was young, each remarried. She lives with her mother and four half-siblings. Her mother worked a night shift, and Diana was expected to raise the children. She was not allowed to date, nor to have anyone over to visit her, male or female. She became extremely anxious and resented the responsibility placed upon her. Her feelings toward her mother became more and more ambivalent—she wanted to be loved by her, but resented her. When she was 12 a friend introduced her to Dexedrine® which she took several days a week. She stole money from her mother to pay for it. She began to sneak out at night after her mother came home, going to parties where beer and marijuana were common. It was desperately important to her that someone like her, and she couldn't tolerate the pressures of home without her "uppers."

When her mother started working another shift Diana began to run away. The third time she was gone long enough to try acid and sex, and continues to pursue both. She stated later that she was hooked on "uppers." She exhibited many problem behaviors—she wouldn't take baths, delighted in talking of bizarre sexual practices, and was caught sniffing gas.

She is an insecure girl who seems to work to make herself unattractive, yet longs to be loved. She literally has no appropriate interpersonal skills because she had few chances to learn them. Fearing rejection, she does not approach other people except in an obnoxious fashion. Her acquaintances continue to be delinquents who pressure her to take drugs, engage in intercourse, and so on. Until she begins to like herself and feel that she is worthy of other friends, there is not much likelihood of change. Her totally restrictive home life has had severe repercussions.

Frequently cognitive structures are inadequately developed in adolescent girls because of academic deficiencies and lack of modeling in homes and community environment. Pressures of biochemical changes and instinctual urges are expressed in the immature behavior of the younger child which leads to more conflict and stress. Failure of the development of cognitive structures leads to a failure or inability to understand and perceive the roles, perspectives and concerns of other people. The girl has extreme difficulty in shifting from one aspect or understanding of a situation to another and from one role to another. This means that she has a great deal of difficulty "putting herself in someone else's shoes" to understand how they might feel in response to her behavior. While she may at times react empathetically, she nonetheless has difficulty perceiving another person's viewpoint.

This situation is reflected in moral judgment. Until the growing youth reaches adolescence, behavior is regulated by restrictions imposed by authority figures. That is, for example, a child will not take things that belong to someone else primarily because she has learned that punishment or immediate undesirable consequences follow. Mature moral judgment comes when the person has advanced cognitively to the point where she can understand the long-term social implications of her behavior. Understanding why it is wrong to steal is much more complex than fearing immediate subsequent punishment. It involves the rights and privileges of living in a society with other people where adherence to the Golden Rule promotes mutual respect of property and other people's rights. The acquisition of self-accepted moral principles or an appreciation for individual rights and how one must respect these rights if they are to be reciprocated depends on learning some rather complex concepts— concepts not acquired by many children until 10 years of age. The rate of acquisition of this conceptual framework is thought to be related to intelligence, learning experiences, and social or cultural backgrounds.

The role and power of the peer group for the adolescent is remarkable. Adolescence is traditionally the period of development when there is a defiance or questioning of parental standards. Conformity to behavior of peers is the "in thing." Peer approval is the most potent reinforcer of behavior. This is a period when the stress and strain of synchronizing differing value systems frequently culminates in acts of juvenile delinquency. The peer group has become an important source of rewards and punishment and a source of behavior to imitate as evidenced in the previously discussed cases of Janet and Joyce. Predominant peer group values may be the same as parents or they may differ. Behaviors in which the adolescent indulges may represent imitation of parents' actual behavior or of the parents' fantasies. A parent who cannot accept his "darker nature" may be unable to lead a daughter to more adaptive procedures for handling her impulses and basic desires. By adolescence the child may be too independent for the parent to control through restrictive or suppressive measures and society may punish through law the behaviors previously controlled by parents and teachers. The child suddenly is faced with social stigmas and the embarrassment which comes from being called a criminal or a delinquent.

Adolescent girls face many problems of role expectations at this time of life. Behaviors which were appropriate for children are no longer appropriate. Preparation for the adult female role is critical. Expectations and behaviors associated with various roles are much more complex, ambiguous, and conflict-ridden for adolescent girls than for boys. This is particularly true in our culture where the female role is changing. There are more alternatives available to a young lady than the mothering role, now that professions, once considered unique to the male, are viable alternatives for females.

A major concern of the adolescent is answers to the questions, "Who am I?" and "What is to become of me?" Answers to these questions in large measure are determined by the aspirations of the adolescent, i.e., what she views as meaningful goals in life. The following are ten factors influencing aspirations of adolescents as shown in the research literature: (1) social class of parents, (2) parents' aspirations, (3) intelligence of the adolescent, (4) emotional adjustment, (5) social status of friends, (6) early school performance, (7) social ability of the parents, (8) special talents for sports and an admired personality, (9) a high need for achievement, and (10) social class composition of the school attended. Deficits and limitations, in these factors are prevalent among delinquent adolescent girls.

The following quote by Erik Erikson (1950) summarizes some of the adolescent's concerns about his identity and answer to the question "Who am I?"

> Adolescence is the age of final establishment of dominant, positive . . . identity. It is then that a future within reach becomes part of a conscious life plan. It is then that the question arises whether or not the future was anticipated in earlier expectations . . . What the . . . growing, rebelling, maturing youths are now primarily concerned with is who and what they are in the eyes of a wider circle of significant people . . .

Identity is a kind of stability of the adolescent's personality as seen by herself and the social group to which she formally or informally belongs. It is essentially her answer to the question "Who am I?" As a general rule, the self-concept does not fluctuate during the adolescent years; however, major encounters with law and negative life experiences can markedly damage one's self-image. All of the case histories cited have noted feelings of worthlessness, of damaged self-image.

Adolescents undergoing drastic maturational changes are subject to some sharp changes in social roles. They experiment with different personal styles, but all seem to fall short of touching the core of their own self-description. Conviction for a crime must surely come as a jolt to the adolescent and certainly serves as a stimulus for reassessment.

The average adolescent is oriented towards the future. Marriage may be a major goal. Girls differ from boys in the range of occupational choices; traditionally a much narrower range is available. Many are interested in being secretaries, nurses, or teachers. They are generally interested in jobs that would be socially pleasant, where they can make friends and meet possible husbands. While the women's role in America may be changing, these conditions likely still persist.

Delinquent girls frequently manifest less interest in these concerns because they have less of a future orientation and are more concerned about the here and now. Marriage may be the major goal. Many are not even aware of the vocational alternatives. They have had little exposure to vocational possibilities and limited perception of themselves, and their potential abilities. Having been accustomed to failure in the academic setting, frequently they feel cut off from the intellectually-stimulating vocations. Once typed by society as "bad girls" they are often unable to change behavior due to the expectations of both peers and adults.

Self-esteem is an individual's evaluation of himself. One's self-esteem may vary from area to area of functioning. For example, one may see oneself as very competent in sports, but very inferior in academic pursuits. Repeated success experiences in an area lead to high self-esteem whereas repeated failures lead to low self-esteem. The general feeling of self-esteem depends on cumulative experiences of obtaining rewards or failures. The usual process is for self-esteem to be more stable in adolescence and less influenced by momentary occurrences. Again the major impact of court experiences may seriously damage the adolescent's self-esteem.

A major difficulty for the adolescent arises from the fact that expectations are ambiguous in our culture. Adults often do not know what to expect of teenagers. Accompanying these ambiguities are associated uncertainties and even conflicts which are a function of the fact that adolescents are neither rewarded or punished very consistently. They are expected to be dependent, yet to be independent; required to earn money yet required to go to school; be sexually desirable, but not engage in sexual behavior; be idealistic but realistic. Each young person must work out for herself the particular role with which she is comfortable. And she is less likely to become delinquent if she does this in an atmosphere of genuine concern and caring. If her parents do not provide this, or provide gifts and immediate gratification of wants rather than limits and love, then a delinquent child is aborning.

Society then helps decide, by its treatment of the behavior, in just which direction the child will go.

BIBLIOGRAPHY

1. Blos, P.: *On Adolescence*. New York, The Free Press, 1962.
2. Erikson, E. H.: *Childhood and Society*. New York, W. W. Norton and Co., 1950.
3. Gold, M. and Douvan, Elizabeth: *Adolescent Development: Readings in Research and Theory*. Boston, Allyn and Bacon Inc., 1969.
4. Mossen, P. H., Conger, J. J. and Kagan, J.: *Child Development and Personality*. New York, Harper and Row, 1969.
5. Stone, L. J. and Church, J.: *Childhood and Adolescence: A Psychology of the Growing Person*, 2nd ed. New York, Random House, 1968.

Chapter 7

THE EFFECTS OF MOOD ALTERING DRUGS: PLEASURES AND PITFALLS

Paul Rosenberg

Introduction

WE LIVE in an age where a nation of young people have been cast adrift, cut off from their elders, to search alone for meaning in a world that often does not make sense. The normal rites of passage have been ruptured. Our children no longer seem able to use the old cultural norms as a yardstick. These valuable traditions, which tie us so richly to the world, are being stripped of their meaning by the increasing speed of social

88

change. Without a cultural inheritance, a young person is forced to grope for direction at a time in his life when his adolescent attachment to utopian goals and his desperate struggle for independence cloud his ability to make mature judgments. In this confusing marketplace of growing up are many drugs; some old and some new, which are able to profoundly affect the depth, intensity, and meaning of our experience of reality and of ourselves.

Nursed by the impersonality of the television set, taught to hide behind the masks of conformity that have become caskets for many of their parents, our young people have been cut off from experiencing their own integralness by the blast of our mass culture. Affluence can have an emptiness as profound as that of a ghetto. People at all levels are starving, searching desperately for anything that allows them the chance to feel better. Drugs, like alcohol, often appear to offer a way out. Drugs can increase one's sensitivity to feelings or they can depress one's internal experience of one's self. They can alter the boredom and plainness that is so much of life. But the more you depend on a pill to feel alive, the less you can feel yourself. The drug becomes a device for stimulation, like masturbation, which gets you away from the real thing. Suddenly, the drug takes over; you become automatized by the need for artificial assistance which diminishes your control over your own world. Reality is not heightened sensitivity. In the confusing search for something real, people often mistake more intense experience for the deeper realities of intimacy and communication. We must avoid trying to frighten people away from the world of drugs. Rather, we must illuminate the problems that drugs create. Then we must trust our youth to explore, experiment and eventually choose their own way, which is indeed the process of growth and maturation.

Drugs are not good or bad. They cannot be eliminated from the American scene. We must face the reality that they are here to stay. This means that we must avoid trying to educate our youth to resist all drugs as evil. In a world where drugs are ubiquitous, we must rely on the ability of youth to choose for themselves, for we cannot protect them. When presenting the facts about drugs and their effects, we must be very careful to point out why drugs are so popular, acknowledging their pleasures as well as their pitfalls. Thus, the viewpoint we present will be realistic and will help to make sense out of the confusion of the drug scene. Our children are desperate for someone they can trust. In focusing on the negative aspects of the world of drugs, in an attempt to protect by fear, we alienate the very ones we want to help. It is only with humility and honesty that we can help to convey the kind of information about drugs that will help others find their own way in the difficult world of growing up today.

Hallucinogens

LSD (*Lysergic Acid Diethylamide*)

LSD is chemically derived from ergot alkaloids. These compounds are found in a fungus of the genus *claviceps*, that occasionally infected wheat in Central Europe. When bread was prepared from this grain, there were outbreaks of ergot poisoning with temporary psychotic behavior. Albert Hoffman, a Swiss chemist, who synthesized LSD in 1937, accidentally ingested some in 1943 and discovered its ability to produce severe distortions of consciousness. LSD remained relatively unknown in the United States until 1959 when a religious group on the West Coast began using it for the induction of mystical states.

Timothy Leary's work at Harvard on LSD began in the early 1960's. Previously, he had been an outstanding psychologist whose personality evaluation procedures are still widely used. His LSD research broke the normal boundaries of academic propriety and led to his expulsion from Harvard. He helped to promulgate the widespread use of LSD, providing many with guidelines on how to handle this powerful psychedelic drug. Concomitantly, the use of marijuana and other drugs increased dramatically, particularly among the white, middle-class. LSD was felt to be a kind of salvation. Adolescents of many ages headed for San Francisco's Haight-Ashbury in the summer of 1967 when the vision of salvation peaked in the world of flower children. Initially, the love culture seemed possible. But soon the pressures of too many mouths to feed and too much hostility turned the once peaceful hippy scene into a dangerous, desolate ghetto. And now many began to demonstrate the poor judgment and mental disorganization that can result from the excessive use of LSD. The drug that "turned on" so many people could also destroy, both by horrifying bad trips and gradual mental deterioration. It is fortunate that of the many millions of Americans who have experimented with LSD, only a few appear to have been seriously damaged by it.

THE ACID EXPERIENCE. An LSD trip can be of a magical or mystical nature, giving one's environment the quality of paradise or it can turn the world into a raging, terrifying inferno. Not only are there altered perceptual effects, but the very meaning of our existence can be called into question. A single LSD trip can totally alter one's direction in life.

The intensity of LSD experience is dose related. The drug produces hypersuggestability. Thus, one's emotional state when taking the drug as well as the environment or setting in which the drug is used are extremely important in determining what kind of trip one has. You can never be sure where you are going. LSD is always a voyage into the unknown. Sometimes a trip begins slowly, with gradual changes in one's perceptual awareness. The intensity of color seems to radiate with greater vividness. The whole world may seem enriched. At other times the experience may start with an explosive force and drop into a mystical, magical, delusional world, where reality changes swiftly. Perceptual alterations, which are usually predominant, involve distortion and changes in perspective rather than true hallucinatory phenomena. At higher doses, hallucinations are more common. Synesthesias, where one sense seems to flow into another, often are reported. Music may seem to touch your body. Depth perception may alter. A plaster wall may seem like mountainous terrain and solid objects may appear to undulate to the rhythm of the music. Sexual orgasms may be experienced in multiple modes.

The ability to estimate the passage of time is altered. With the rapid flow of experiential events, the individual on LSD feels a great deal of time must have passed. Five minutes may seem like hours. Thought processes are loosened during and often following the LSD experience. Associations may become more fanciful and one's judgment is seriously impaired by magical, illogical thinking. Ego integration may dissolve, causing extreme panic states. Part of traveling safely with LSD involves being able to tolerate new states of ego disorientation without fear. One needs the ability to stay calm, while feeling a loss of connection to the body and normal ego boundaries.

Beyond the usual acid trip is the possibility of religious experience. Mystical states occur spontaneously and have been reported since Biblical times. LSD sessions occasionally have similar, if not identical, transcendental qualities. People describe seeing the Godhead or the golden radiance of God. Usually the experience is related to one's religious background and is remembered as a deeply moving religious event.

PANICS AND "BUMMERS." The increased intensity with which LSD allows us to voyage into our innermost feelings also can carry us to the depths of terror. Frequently during an LSD trip, there are brief periods when one feels afraid. If the response to this fear is running away or increased anxiety, one can create a terrifying and overwhelming crisis. For those who have taken LSD numerous times, the first encounter with the extreme terror of an LSD "bummer" frequently motivates them to stop taking the drug permanently.

Panic experiences of ego disorganization are sometimes somaticized; it is as if one is dead, that the rest of the world is dead, that one's body is coming apart, or magically bleeding to death. "Bummers" are experienced both interpersonally and intrapersonally. In a group, the heightened suggestability of the LSD state may cause one to feel that unrelated movements of others are meant as signs of an impending attack. The paranoia may grow rapidly until it involves everything. Feelings of depersonalization or unreality become overwhelming. The more one fights or flees from the paranoia, the more frantic and intense it becomes. Suddenly there does not seem to be any hope. Out of this desperation comes the frantic terror and panic of an LSD "bummer."

Often people are severely shaken and are left with intense anxiety for weeks following a bad trip. A person can often be talked down from a "bummer" by an experienced guide. Getting an individual to focus on his breathing helps to orient him and reassure him that his body is still intact. One can remind him that he is taking a drug which accounts for the experience he is having. The firm, commanding, reassuring voice of an experienced guide, helping the individual to understand what is happening, is enough to bring most people down. When someone cannot be talked down in such a manner, any of the major antipsychotic tranquilizers are rapidly effective. Some researchers have suggested that the use of tranquilizers may increase the likelihood of flashbacks.

CHANGES IN DIRECTION. One's conception of what is important in life is developed in our early years, matures in adolescence and usually remains stable throughout our adult life. These assumptions are rarely thought about and remain as unconscious determinants of what we want and how we behave. LSD can cause rapid and major changes in these basic feelings which can change totally the way a person chooses to live. To illustrate this, let us briefly review two case histories.

Tom, when brought into a county hospital by his parents, was a nineteen-year-old young man who had been going to college. For the past year and a half he had been taking LSD during weekly beer parties on the beach with his fraternity brothers. He continued to go to school, did better than average work and lived at home. His parents were unaware of the fact that he was taking LSD. His lifestyle remained unchanged. Approximately six months before he was brought to the hospital, he was picked up while hitchhiking by a group of hippies. He accompanied them to their commune where he took LSD. On his first trip with this familial group, he experienced profound new sensations. Their caring and sensitive relationships gave him his first deep awareness that he wanted more intimacy than he had known previously. When he returned home, he quit college which he now saw as a useless waste of time. He gave away his clothes and refused to wear shoes. His parents felt desperate as he was planning to leave home permanently to join his hippy friends.

His family never had a great deal of internal cohesiveness. They were relatively stable but rarely related emotionally. Tom had never had any of the important experiences at home that he was able to have in his new relationships. Though he was unrealistic, he was not psychotic. He had changed his values so enormously that he could no longer remain within the sphere of his earlier upbringing.

In another case, a young "straight" salesman took LSD for the first time with his girlfriend. During his first and only trip, this isolated young man experienced such tremendous warmth and tenderness from his girlfriend that he was overwhelmed by previously unknown feelings of love and affection. He decided that his past way of life no longer made sense. After the trip, he quit his job, and went to work for a community organization which assisted young people who were having problems with drugs.

Such enormous changes in lifestyles do not always occur. Less pronounced changes are more common. Some individuals attempt to maintain their LSD heightened level of awareness after their trip. This leads to bizarre or unusual behavior, expressing their dissatisfaction with normal, comparatively mundane reality. In their search to reestablish the beautific vision experienced on LSD, some may temporarily lose their ability to make appropriate judgments. They act as if the world had been transformed and they may place untenable demands on the people around them. They may ask "why? Why do I need a car, or new clothes, when simple things are really enough?" This is indeed simplistic thinking, but one cannot challenge it with ordinary logic. For unless a person wants to work for certain values, one cannot force it on him. People are very willing to give up a job or a way of life for a vision of something that seems much more important.

This has happened to many. It may be one of the reasons for the dramatic change of values we see in the counter-culture. And perhaps, in the long run, we might be wise to consider where the mad rush of progress is taking us; whether the natural pleasures of seeing the world in fresh, simple ways are not sometimes missed by our sophisticated, appliance-using society.

FLASHBACKS AND PSYCHOSES. The dangerous consequences of post-LSD reactions are rare. Considering the tremendous power of the

LSD experience this is quite fortunate. Yet for the few who go through the terrors of repeated flashbacks or who become psychotic, an LSD trip can spell disaster. Most people recover from these sequelae, but some will remain in our state hospitals for long periods of time.

Flashbacks occur when unresolved psychic trauma is partially brought to awareness but incompletely dealt with during a trip. It is like opening Pandora's Box just a bit and not being able to seal it tight again. Later, some event jars the box just enough to open it briefly. With the dread contents exposed to awareness, even in the unconscious mind, the disorientation of the LSD state flashes back suddenly. Eventually, one's psychological defenses return and normal reality is reestablished. Flashbacks can be treated by psychotherapy, by repeated use of LSD in a treatment setting or by major tranquilizers. Insight-oriented psychotherapy is the treatment of choice but may take a number of years. Flashbacks frequently cease spontaneously. Flashbacks can occur with full-blown psychotic hallucinatory effects or they may appear as only mild perceptual changes. Marijuana and other drugs can precipitate them as can emotional experiences and anxiety. Other post-LSD reactions include depression, chronic anxiety states, prolonged visual effects, and paranoia.

Psychotic reactions requiring hospitalization are a consequence of using LSD in only a very small percentage of cases. Such individuals most frequently have schizophrenic decompensations or, more rarely, prolonged hallucinosis. Usually such psychotic states resolve slowly with therapy. LSD is most likely to cause psychotic reactions in individuals who have rigid defenses which are crucial to their stability or who have had previous schizophrenic illness. Well integrated individuals almost never have any of these prolonged disasterous effects, despite the fact that they too can have frightening LSD "bummers."

One syndrome that is similar to an LSD flashback is the repeated experience of being "stoned" (i.e. confused, anxious and disoriented) which occurs in some individuals who have rigid defenses against their angry and destructive impulses. If they have any drug experience, from LSD to marijuana, which loosens their defensive control of their enormous anger, they become unable to tolerate even the mildest of anxiety-producing or threatening situations. They feel "stoned" or dazed as they attempt to control their unacceptable feelings. It is much the same feeling of overwhelming confusion and disorientation that normal individuals might have briefly in reaction to a catastrophe. This feeling of being "stoned" is persistent and may last with variable intensity for years. It is aggravated by the omnipotently demanding, passive-aggressive personality style that is most frequently seen in this syndrome. Psychotherapy for this condition is often prolonged and difficult.

It is a wonder that so many severely disturbed people who have taken LSD and other psychedelics have not become more bizarre or disturbed. Perhaps, the accepting, loosely structured, undemanding quality of the underground community allows disorganized individuals to function without drawing attention to themselves. It is not clear why LSD will increase the mental disability of some individuals and not others.

PHYSIOLOGIC CONSIDERATIONS. LSD is one of the most potent chemicals known. Merely 25 micrograms of this drug can cause a change in one's inner awareness. Usually, doses range from 100 to 500 micrograms, although intake of up to 2,000 to 4,000 micrograms have been reported. The trip lasts from 6 to 12 hours with its peak occurring during the first 2 to 4 hours. For most people, tolerance will begin to develop after a single dose and may take 4 to 8 days to wear off. Cross tolerance exists between most psychedelics including LSD, mescaline and psilocybin. Experiments have shown that these drugs cannot be distinguished experientially by experienced users.

LSD has many sympathomimetic effects, most pronounced of which is pupillary dilation of up to 6 millimeters. Minor elevation in blood pressure and temperature occur, as well as muscular weakness, numbness, tremulousness, tachycardia and mild hyperglycemia. The nonspecific stress of the LSD state produces increased adrenocortical steroids. Eosinophilia and leukocytosis also can be observed. Electroencephalographic tracings show diminished amplitude and low voltage fast waves with increased desynchrony. Periods of dreaming during sleep are prolonged for the 24 to 48 hours following an LSD experience.

The mode of action of LSD remains speculative. Naturally occurring neurologically active amines such as serotonin and norepinephrine show chemical structures similar to most of the psychoactive drugs. Hallucinogenic agents may compete with and block or possibly facilitate synaptic transmissions.

LSD has been involved in a great controversy involving possible chromosomal damage. Unfortunately, these studies have utilized subjects who have had multi-drug exposure. Nevertheless, there is clear cut evidence that LSD does increase the number of chromosomal breaks and crossovers. Chromosomal changes appear three times more frequently in LSD users than in control groups. These changes are similar to those induced by radiation, viruses, and other mutagens. There is evidence suggesting that LSD can cross the placenta increasing the chromosomal changes in the fetus. However, from the epidemiological point of view, LSD only rarely has been implicated in congenital birth defects. The effects on germ cells still have to be evaluated. We can conclude only that we do not know the consequences of the chromosomal changes that are observed with LSD use. We must proceed with caution until adequate data is available.

CLINICAL USES. Research work on LSD remains in its infancy. A number of studies already have shown some promise for LSD as a therapeutic agent. Patients on the verge of death after a protracted and painful illness, such as cancer, usually experience a great deal of anxiety and terror. With proper preparation, an LSD session can substantially change their perspective on their impending death. Most feel more accepting about the inevitability of death. Additionally, LSD has been shown to decrease pain in chronically ill cancer patients and to increase the effectiveness of opiates.

LSD has proven to be of some value in the treatment of alcoholics. More than half of the alcoholics treated with one to three high dose sessions of LSD have shown improvement. Reports from Eastern and Western Europe and the United States suggest that LSD may be a useful adjunct in insight-oriented psychotherapy. Combined with regular therapy sessions, LSD experiences inhibit ego defenses and allow for the recall of primitive fantasies and traumatic memories not usually available to the conscious mind. LSD enhances emotional abreactions. Reports from psychoanalytic researchers using LSD suggest that even the earliest of traumas, the pain of being born, has somatic traces which can be re-experienced. Claims have been made for the value of LSD in treating both schizophrenia and neurotic patients. These experiments bear further study as LSD could well become an important addition to the armamentarium of psychotherapeutic drugs.

Other Hallucinogens

Mescaline (3, 4, 5,-Trimethoxyphenylethylamine)

Mescaline, one of the alkaloids present in the peyote cactus which grows in the Sonoran deserts of the American Southwest and Mexico, has long been used by Indians as a part of religious rituals. In these ceremonies the adult men of the tribe sit through the night after chewing peyote buttons, having visions and singing peyote songs.

Mescaline, the active alkaloid of peyote, is chemically related to epinephrine. It was studied in the early 1950's and received much popular attention. Peyote has an intensely bitter taste and often causes nausea and vomiting. Trips on peyote tend to last 12 to 24 hours while mescaline lasts 6 to 8 hours. Many drug users feel that mescaline produces a psychedelic experience that has more colorful, gentle somatic qualities than LSD and is less likely to be terrifying. In contradiction, research work has shown that people are unable to differentiate between the effects of most psychedelics.

Psilocybin and Psilocin (dimethyl-4-phosphoryltryptamine and dimethyl-4-hydroxyltryptamine)

The psychoactive alkaloids found in the Mexican mushroom, psilocybe mexicana heim, is also used by Indians in Mexico to produce religious visions. Psilocin is slightly more potent than psilocybin. Both produce states indistinguishable from LSD, but have a duration of approximately 3 to 6 hours. They are rarely, if ever, available on the street, although preparations of other substances are frequently sold as psilocybin.

DMT (dimethoxytryptamine) and DET (diethyltryptamine)

DMT often has been called the businessman's acid trip as it produces rapid hallucinogenic effects which last 10 to 30 minutes. It is inactive when taken orally. Usually people smoke DMT, either by heating the crystals and inhaling the vapors or by dipping marijuana into a solution of DMT. It has a strong, acrid metallic odor. It can be sniffed or injected. Intramuscular injections can cause a tight, choking sensation in the chest and brief periods of unconsciousness followed by intense hallucinations. DMT occurs in the seeds of *Piptadenia peregrina* which are used in South America to make *Cohoba* snuff. DMT has autonomic effects similar to LSD. DET is a synthetic preparation which psychoactive properties resemble DMT.

Lysergic Acid Amide

The wild American morning glory has four species which produce seeds containing lysergic acid amide and isolysergic acid amide. The potency varies with each batch of seeds. The seeds are pulverized and taken orally, often producing a lethargic, dreamy state with frequent nausea and vomiting. Hallucinations occur at high doses close to the point where ergot toxicity is observed.

STP (2, 5, dimethoxy-4-methylamphetamine)

STP is a synthetic hallucinogen that recently has come directly from the experimental laboratory into street use. It was alleged to precipitate frequent "bummers" and last 1 to 2 days. However, larger than normal amounts were used, probably accounting for these misconceptions. It is thought to be about as potent as psilocibin.

The Peace Pill—PCP

PCP is an animal tranquilizer known as phencyclidine (Sernyl®). First making its appearance in the summer of 1967 as "the peace pill" in San Francisco, PCP received a lot of attention and was known to cause frequent bad trips. Some find it enjoyable at first, but there have been repeated reports of acute paranoia and "bummers." Known as "angel dust," it is sprayed on marijuana or parsley and sold as an hallucinogen. It usually produces a greater disorganization of the thought process than LSD. Feelings of unreality are also common. It can be identified frequently by the heavy chemical odor that lingers in the air when it is smoked. A cheap chemical, which apparently is easily obtained, it is frequently sold as LSD, mescaline, or THC. At times it may be added to other drugs to boost their effect. The quality and potency of drugs obtained on the street are always unknown. Strychnine and other poisons have been found both alone and as contaminants of such drugs.

Marijuana and Hashish

Marijuana is the common name given to the dried leaves and flowers of the hemp plant, *cannabis sativa*. Hashish is made from the dried resins of the same plant, or the Indian variety, *cannabis indicus*. Hashish is more potent but contains the same active chemical, tetrahydracarbaminol (THC). It can be classified as an hallucinogen since, in adequate amounts, THC produces hallucinations.

HISTORICAL CONSIDERATIONS. *Cannabis indicus* has been used in India for centuries for religious, pleasurable, and medicinal purposes. In 1839, W. B. O'Shaughnessey published an article, "On the Preparations of the Indian Hemp," which first introduced the therapeutic possibilities of cannabis into Western medicine. O'Shaughnessey had been serving with the British Army in India. He suggested that hemp might be useful in producing analgesia, as an anticonvulsant, and as a muscle relaxant. His report generated a great deal of attention. By 1860 the Ohio State Medical Society's committee on *cannabis indicus* reported success in treating pain, childbirth, coughs, psychoses, and insomnia using this new drug. In 1889, E. A. Birch reported in *Lancet* that Indian hemp could be used in treating opiate addiction. A year later, in 1890, J. R. Reynolds reported in *Lancet* on 30 years of clinical experience using cannabis. He observed that Cannabis was useful as a sedative and was valuable for various neuralgias, migraine headache, and numerous nervous conditions including depression. He warned against overdose, noting the necessity to titrate the quantity given to each patient. Even the great American physician, William Osler, in his 1916 edition of his textbook of medicine wrote, concerning migraine headaches, "*Cannabis indicus* is probably the most satisfactory remedy."

Indian hemp was used extensively by physicians throughout the latter half of the 19th and early part of the 20th centuries. Hemp was a frequent component of over-the-counter nerve and cough cures. In 1937 the marijuana tax act put an end to the common use of cannabis for medicinal purposes. This occurred over the objections of the American Medical Association who protested that it was a useful drug.

Since the 1920's, the use and distribution of marijuana through the fringe or criminal element of our society has given it a reputation for being associated with criminal behaviour and violent crimes. The La Guardia report and many recent studies have disproved this association. Yet there remains a widespread misconception that the use of marijuana presages a moral degeneration and eventual addiction to heroin.

WHY DO PEOPLE LIKE MARIJUANA? The tremendously rapid increase in the use of marijuana throughout all levels of our culture is surely the most striking drug phenomenon of the past decade. Studies have shown that from 50 percent to 80 percent of our college students have used or use marijuana. Of course, only a few use it daily. Yet, more and more people seem to find it an enjoyable and relaxing pastime. One young man describes his feelings this way, "The thing about it is that it makes me feel whole; grass is like a wholeness where you can still function but still have that all-in-one enjoyable feeling." Many have found that marijuana is a valuable tranquilizer. It can take away the feeling of emptiness and insecurity. It can create a delicious timelessness in which the mind seems more awake and the world particularly vibrant and meaningful.

During one's first encounter with marijuana, some individuals experience nothing out of the ordinary. Anxiety about smoking grass for the first time can completely shut off the effects of the drug at moderate dosage. For others, the intensity of the new perceptions can be overwhelming. The changes in time and spatial dimension, the clarity and depth of feeling that are often reached are profound experiences. Marijuana and hashish are usually smoked, but they can also be taken in the form of an alcohol extract or, more frequently, mixed in foods, such as brownies or cookies.

Usually marijuana is used as a means to foster social communication, much as alcohol is used socially. By passing a "joint" around and turning on together, an immediate comraderie is established, particularly since smoking marijuana is still illegal. Under these circumstances people often find it easier to relate and be involved. As people become more intoxicated, they tend to become increasingly withdrawn into their fantasies and reveries, thus cutting down on interpersonal communication. When alone, people tend to use the drug to decrease anxiety, to speed up their mental processes and to enjoy its somatic effects. The ability of the marijuana high to ameliorate feelings of anxiety, emotional pain and loneliness perhaps best explains why so many repeatedly turn to this drug experience. Marijuana is liked because it helps in feeling better; it is replacing alcohol as the drug of choice of today's young people.

PHYSIOLOGICAL EFFECTS. The ability of marijuana to produce psychological and physiological effects varies with its THC content. The percentage of THC usually present in marijuana available on the streets is less than one percent. Panic, hallucinatory and dissociative reactions can occur when more potent preparations are available.

Initially, the drug causes drowsiness, dryness of the mouth and weakly dilates blood vessels producing injected conjunctiva. Tachycardias, slight decreases in blood pressure, and pupilary dilation are common. Transient hypoglycemia often causes a craving for sweets. This hypoglycemic response disappears with more chronic use. At higher doses there is a diffuse depressant effect on the central nervous system. A dreamy, lethargic state occurs where inhibitions are decreased. Impairment of immediate memory, increased suggestibility, shortened attention span, fragmentation of thought, synesthesias, altered sense perceptions and moderate ataxia are all aspects of the "high" of marijuana intoxication. This hypnogogic state has qualities similar to the sedative experiences during the induction of anesthesia as well as the psychedelic experience with LSD. Coordination studies in driving automobiles have demonstrated that intoxication with moderate doses of marijuana does not impair driving skills. Higher drug levels cause difficulties with attention and perception that makes driving hazardous.

Partial tolerance develops with chronic marijuana use. Tolerant individuals often find their "high" periods shortened with fewer perceptual changes. However, the timeless, tranquilizing and comforting qualities usually remain. Tolerance disappears 3 to 5 days after drug use stops. Marijuana is not addicting. Severe psychological dependence results when individuals depend on grass to relieve their anxiety and frustrations. There are no problems in withdrawing from marijuana. Only occasional heavy users have periods of restlessness and anxiety. Most people use it in their spare time to induce a mild euphoria. With this kind of use, psychological dependence usually does not become a problem. Morning hangovers are infrequently encountered. Yet some individuals may have these regularly. They report fatigue, lethargy, mild to moderate confusion and dissociative feelings. No fatalities have been reported from an overdose of marijuana. The drug, when smoked, is automatically self-titrated. If the user becomes excessively intoxicated, he finds himself unable to continue smoking and thus discontinues his drug intake.

PSYCHOLOGICAL CHANGES. During a marijuana high, one experiences a rapid flow of thoughts and associations. Often one is able to hear or feel impulses from different parts of one's self that are normally repressed. The vicious, silly, childish, or self-disapproving voices within may be clearly heard. Often one takes the role of a spectator looking at one's own feelings and reactions. There is a general enhancement of the prevailing mood. Hostile or angry feelings are usually modified or lost entirely. An individual who is "stoned" may be aware of the intensity with which he is able to perceive the external reality. There is a change in the quality of reality, as if the veil of one's anxieties were lifted and perception were sharpened. Alternately, one may feel cut off and fragmented producing severe paranoia.

The marijuana high can be focused both externally or internally. One can go from the internal to the external experience rapidly. Frequently, people state that they have had to respond to external reality such as a knock on the door or being stopped by a policeman. They note that they can appropriately orient themselves except when extremely intoxicated. This control is an unusual quality of marijuana intoxication.

It often has been stated that marijuana acts as an aphrodisiac. Basically, this is true, although it does not appear to be in itself a sexual stimulant. Instead, the aphrodisiac qualities of marijuana seem to be due to its ability to remove inhibitions and allow one to focus intensely on the pleasures of sexual sensations.

The syndrome of the heavy marijuana abuser is only beginning to be understood. He tends to be an individual who feels very inadequate and uses intellectual defenses to avoid his painful feelings. The prolonged use of marijuana creates a kind of distance from the world. One observes what is happening rather than participating with feelings and reactions. This withdrawal includes a loss of interest in others as well as a lessened concern for the propriety of social norms. The chronic marijuana user has a sluggish, even flowing, almost mechanized walk that can be identified by a keen observer. He tends to neglect his body and there is a loss of general alertness. He seems to be far away and often demonstrates clearly confused or loosened thought process. Delusional or obsessional ideation may be present. No longer does it seem meaningful to hold a job or complete school. This lack of involvement has been called the *amotivation syndrome*. Most of these symptoms are reversible when the individual stops abusing marijuana.

ADVERSE REACTIONS. Varying degrees of mild paranoid or fragmented feelings are commonly reported. These disappear as the drug wears off and require no treatment. Acute and chronic psychoses develop only rarely; they develop most frequently in rigid, schizoid individuals. These may require long term psychotherapy and tranquilizers. In chronic psychoses, particularly with marginal but functioning individuals, it may be difficult to get them to give up using marijuana. They have come to rely on its tranquilizing effects and do not connect their disorganization with the use of the drug.

Stimulants

Amphetamines

Amphetamines are a class of drugs which act as stimulants of the central nervous system. Their use and abuse extends throughout all levels of our culture, from the truck driver who takes a "bennie" to stay alert on the road to the housewife who needs her morning diet pill to keep up with the rapid pace of everyday life. It is little wonder that the youth subculture had adopted amphetamines as a frequently used, though less frequently abused, form of stimulation.

Amphetamines were prepared first in 1887 but did not become clinically available until 1930 when the sympathomimetic effects of amphetamines began to be compared to those of epinephrine. They were not used frequently until the second World War. There are a number of amphetamines including amphetamine (Benzedrine®), dextro-amphetamine (Dexedrine®), methamphetamine (Desoxyn® or Methadrine®). Combinations such as Obetrol® are used to decrease the unwanted side-effects of nervousness and irritability.

PHARMACOLOGICAL EFFECTS. Amphetamines function as a stimulant of both the motor and sensory aspects of the central nervous system. They produce an alert, awake feeling of confidence and potency and facilitate task oriented behavior for 4 to 6 hours. Amphetamines stimulate heart function with the heart rate increasing proportionately to the dose of the drug. Increased irritability and increased perception of auditory stimuli are also dose related. At high doses, toxic psychoses develop with visual and auditory illusions, delusions and hallucinations having extremely paranoid characteristics. Sexual interest often is increased on the intellectual level but the physical ability to perform may be reduced.

The pharmacological evidence suggests that amphetamines act through multiple pathways involving catecholamine metabolism, monamine oxidase inhibition and by direct intrinsic effect. The dose of amphetamines needed to produce toxic psychotic effects varies tremendously. Chronic oral or intravenous use of 100–500 mg. per day usually precipitates psychosis but individuals have tolerated well over 1,000 mg. per day without toxic signs. While not addicting, amphetamines are extremely habituating, producing profound psychological dependence. Withdrawal from the drug produces tenseness, tremors and anxiety culminating in moderate to extreme depression. People develop rapid tolerance to the effects of amphetamines so that the drug no longer remains effective unless the dose is constantly increased. With large repeated doses taken intravenously damage and loss of brain cells occurs. It is surprising, however, that despite tremendously heavy amphetamine abuse, most individuals ultimately show only minimal functional brain damage. There are recent reports of a new syndrome where inflammation and damage to blood vessels are seen in association with intravenous amphetamine abuse. There is a significant increase in cerebrovascular accidents (strokes) in these patients.

The rate of metabolism of amphetamines is relatively slow. Usually the body takes 2 to 3 days to eliminate a single dose of the drug. Much is excreted unchanged in the urine which facilitates detection when a question of toxicity arises.

AMPHETAMINE SYNDROMES. The mildest form of amphetamine abuse has been common throughout all levels of society, from students to housewives. It is usually iatrogenic and consists of the daily use of low dosages of amphetamines from 10 to 60 mg per day. Physicians have been in the practice of prescribing amphetamines for weight gain and other symptoms of depression. Amphetamines reverse mild depression for a time, but due to the rapid tolerance that develops, individuals who begin using moderate or low doses of the drug soon find that this does not meet their needs. Slowly, they must increase the amount they take to get the same kind of effect. Many overlook the basic euphoria and sense of powerfulness that goes along with amphetamine use, believing instead that they are taking the amphetamines for weight reduction, or because the doctor prescribed it. As increasing amounts are used, insomnia often results. Fatigued in the morning, they again have to increase their intake to get through the next day. As they begin taking higher and higher doses, suspicious feelings erupt into their consciousness. They believe that people are against them. Numerous frightening perceptual experiences occur which are interpreted in a paranoid manner. There is a tremendous lability of affect with great and frantic mood swings. Thus, the physician who prescribes amphetamines freely can unwittingly convert a patient's mild depression into a toxic psychosis. At best, he can help his patient become habituated to amphetamines rather than dealing with their underlying depressed feelings.

Intravenous use of amphetamines is relatively rare. It is restricted to a very small group of individuals whose feelings of inadequacy are so extreme that they leave the individual with a total sense of powerlessness. The experience of an injection of intravenous amphetamines gives such an individual an incredible sense of power and potency. They rapidly become habituated. Usually the drug is taken in "runs," lasting several days, in which the person does not sleep, rarely eats, and takes the drug as frequently as possible, usually every 2 to 6 hours. As the drug is injected, the user experiences a sudden euphoria (a flash or a rush) which is felt as an explosive orgasmic aliveness of the body and mind. It is an extremely pleasurable sensation to feel alive when your normal state of existence is one of helplessness and apathy. Most users feel that their intellectual functioning is dramatically increased. Some write great poetic pieces, songs or long drafts of manifestos to save the world.

Usually, amphetamine abusers take this drug intravenously in small groups. Often, after the initial rush there is a great deal of talkative communication and activity. As the abuse continues, this activity takes more bizarre and paranoid forms. One "speed freak" couple had strings throughout their apartment forming a kind of spider-web on which they would hang pictures of various objects. Their paranoia caused them to lock their door with six different locks. Like other habitual users, they tolerated a great deal of filth in their "pad" and took very poor care of their bodies.

When amphetamine abusers appear for help, they often are either acutely paranoid or seriously depressed after a long run. They may be suffering from vitamin deficiency and malnutrition. It is both this neglect and the physiological damage to the body and brain that is responsible for the well known slogan "Speed Kills."

TREATMENT CONSIDERATIONS. Toxic psychosis with hallucinations require the use of anti-psychotic drugs. Panic reactions or anxiety attacks can usually be treated with sedatives or minor tranquilizers such as Valium®. Usually, amphetamine abusers have not had sufficient nutrition for a long time and require vitamins and a well balanced diet. The depression that follows abuse of amphetamines is best treated with regular exercise and rest. Amphetamine abusers are extremely difficult to rehabilitate because of their severe personality problems. Until they can develop a sense of competence and usefulness, they frequently return to amphetamines as a way out of their intolerable emotional world.

Cocaine

Cocaine is a potent stimulant. It was used by the Incas of South America as a stimulant for runners in their postal system. By chewing cocoa leaves, the couriers were able to stimulate their physical abilities much as trainers today use amphetamines to push athletes or horses to greater performance. Cocaine, often called "snow," is a preferred drug by the upper-middle class drug players of today's scene.

The use of cocaine to treat morphine addiction began around 1880. Even Sigmund Freud, in 1884, recommended cocaine for neurasthenia and morphinism, insisting that cocaine was non-addicting. As one story goes, Freud was apprehensive when going to social gatherings and would often take cocaine to increase his sense of well-being. This continued only briefly until he observed its addictive potential.

PHYSIOLOGIC EFFECTS. Cocaine stimulates the central nervous system. It appears to potentiate sympathetic nervous functions, perhaps by inhibiting the uptake of norepinephrine at transmitter sites. It is a potent anesthetic of moist surfaces, such as the eye, mouth and throat. When repeatedly applied to mucosal surfaces, it produces severe vascular constriction resulting in local necrosis.

Cocaine is addicting but less rapidly than opiates. Its potential for creating a feeling of competence leads to psychological dependence more rapidly than physiological addiction. Although addicting, withdrawal symptoms are more like those of amphetamines rather than heroin. They include tenseness, muscle ache, mild nausea, general somatic discomfort, anxiety, restlessness and depression. Heavy cocaine abuse, which occurs rarely, often produces severe paranoid psychoses in which the abuser frequently feels that there are small animals or bugs which he must continue to pick off his skin.

Cocaine is a well-loved drug by many who enjoy its ability to induce a sense of power and excitement that is difficult to obtain even with amphetamines. The problem users have with cocaine is that its effects are very short lasting, usually only 30 to 60 minutes. Then there is a prolonged come-down period of 3 to 6 hours during which there is mild to marked somatic discomfort.

THE USE OF COCAINE. Cocaine is rapidly absorbed through the nasal mucosa. Many sniff this drug, often using a dollar bill rolled up to form a narrow tube which allows them to inhale the cocaine crystals past the hairs in their outer nose. The effects are felt rapidly but without a "rush." With extended use, vasoconstriction produces damage to the nasal mucosa. Eventually, a hole in the nasal septum may occur due to the slow erosion of nasal tissue.

Intravenous use of cocaine produces a flash of sexual and physical excitement which is extremely intense. It is a fantastically pleasurable sensation. However, the flash and high are brief so that repeated doses are needed to prevent the uncomfortable come-down. For this reason, cocaine is often combined with other drugs, frequently heroin. This combination is called a "speed-ball." It has both the stimulatory euphoric effect of cocaine while it has the softening and soothing qualities of heroin.

Narcotics

Smack (Heroin), A Seductive Curse

Heroin is the king of drugs. It is the seductive but miserable mistress for the many people who have to hide from the depression and anguish of their own experience of themselves. Heroin is king because it leaves you floating on a calm sea where nothing seems to matter and everything is okay. It is the beautific world of peaceful fantasy where your mind swims in the warm, comfortable, somatic sensation of being held, without pain, and protected from the concerns and worries that make up your life. Suddenly the emptiness disappears. The great, gaping hole that hurts, which you had to hide from everyone, is gone; the terrible gnawing inadequacy has vanished. And in its place is the power and comfort that's called confidence. No one can get to you when you keep "nodding."

Heroin is not a harmful drug. It can be taken for years with almost no physically deleterious effects. Its major side-effects are constipation and, for some men, impotence. It is the great seducer because it makes one feel so good. It is better than psychotherapy or sexuality. It creates a state unlike reality where there is total safety. But heroin, like any narcotic or depressant, is an anesthetizer. It depresses the feeling world and erases from experience the very sensations which are needed to touch life. For many people whose pain is intense, heroin, they feel, is the only way to maintain a constructive lifestyle. Musicians and artists often have turned to heroin to avoid their agony and thus continue their productiveness. Many manage to continue in good health and remain employed for many years. Indeed, if it were not for the intense prejudice against the drug, the rapid tolerance that develops, the dangers of overdose, and for the consequences of non-sterile intravenous injections, heroin might well become the tranquilizing drug of choice for those who suffer from incapacitating anxiety. Unfortunately, the major traumatic effect of heroin is the problem of obtaining it in our society. Having to score daily, with their arms eating up countless dollars causes the addict to be a slave to his body's craving for heroin.

On first exposure, heroin usually produces nausea. By the second or third dose, the nausea disappears. Then heroin is pure pleasure, at least for awhile. Pleasant dreams and fantasies obliterate life's difficulties. Within a few days, tolerance develops so that more heroin is needed to get high. Soon, each day is spent trying to "cop" enough stuff to stay normal. Rarely, if ever, is heroin encountered whose quality and supply is good enough to really get off. The desperate slavery causes the gradual erosion of self-respect. This loss is often bespoken by the ease with which an addict will relate the one thing he hasn't done; it is with this that he retains his last glimmer of self-respect. He has lied, cheated, conned and maneuvered, but perhaps he has not stolen or she has not been a whore.

It is the economic pressure of the heroin scene that causes so many to lose their souls. As slaves in an environment where heroin is expensive and illegal, a whole generation of young addicted people are being forced by their society and their addiction to become criminals. It is an unfortunate sign of our culture's callousness that so many of us look on sick, dependent, disordered addicts as evil degenerates.

The English experience of giving drug users carefully supervised maintenance programs of heroin has proved that heroin itself is not necessarily a detrimental drug. They have shown that narcotic addicts can be stabilized with the official administration of this drug. Americans are beginning to experiment with methadone maintenance which is proving enormously successful.

Whether we like the moral consequences or not we must consider the fact that there are large numbers of people in our country who feel so desperate that they go out of their way, often destroying their entire lives, to take heroin. Normal habits are essential to our functioning. We get into the habit of getting up early to get to work on time. Habits are hard to break. Once someone has become habituated to living in a world where pain is not confronted and experienced, it may be impossible for him to return to the often uncomfortable realities of life. Perhaps we must learn to accept the continuing need for maintenance therapy as a necessary compromise.

A HABIT IS GETTING OFF. With a rope, tie, belt or old nylon stocking you stop the circulation from your shaking, sweating arm. You decide which of your well scarred veins you have a chance of hitting; then you slip in the needle attached to the eyedropper with the rubber bulb on the end. Releasing the pressure lightly from the bulb you anxiously look for the red glob of blood in the bottom of the dropper which means you've got a "register." You've got to be sure you're in the vein before you inject the stuff. If you miss, you get another abscess. The sickness hurts in your bones, your nose is running and you hurt so much you almost wish you were dead. With a slow push it's in and within a few seconds you're beginning to feel normal again. Your dilated pupils become very small. Your confidence is back; you're all right for a few hours before the sickness begins to come again.

Most addicts rarely get high from heroin. Their increasing tolerance to the drug usually prevents them from getting enough to get them off. Their shooting just prevents them from feeling sick. Most addicts could withdraw in 5 to 10 days if they really wanted to. This rarely happens because of their fear of being sick, as well as their lack of commitment of getting clean. Most have become so accustomed to using heroin to avoid problems and have so little to look forward to that they really do not want to give up the relief of their addiction. Moreover, today's street heroin is so diluted that most addicts are addicted to minimal amounts of heroin and have, objectively speaking, mild withdrawal problems.

The variability in the quality of street junk exists in all types of drugs. If an addict scores a few bags of "pure shit" he can accidentally overdose himself causing severe respiratory depression and death. The variety of substances used to cut junk, which then get injected intravenously, add to the dangers of heroin abuse.

It is important to understand that there are many kinds of heroin addicts. In today's drug world we are seeing more of the young addicts whose heroin experiences are recent (under 2 years). Such an addict usually has a greater chance of returning to the social world he came from, not having burned the many bridges that the chronic, long-term addict has already destroyed. The young addict of today is occasionally able to give up heroin with relative ease. He has a non-addicted lifestyle he has not completely forgotten.

It is hoped that the rehabilitative process will take into consideration the relatively new phenomenon of today's "young addict." There is a need for withdrawal and support facilities for young people who can return to a non-addicted way of life. The more severely addicted or chronic addict usually needs long-term maintenance therapy. Occasionally, after years of rehabilitation, a stress-producing situation may trigger an addict's need for heroin. Habits return with lightening speed. Just shooting a day or two is enough to revive the intense need for heroin that initially took 2 to 3 weeks to develop. An important part of treating addiction is to provide addicts with withdrawal assistance when they have reverted to heroin in a period of stress. We must be willing to help the addict in times of crisis, offering him the kind of support that will enable him to find better ways of handling stressful feelings.

Depressants

The Red Devils

Barbiturates, particularly secobarbitol (Seconol® or "reds"), are frequently abused drugs, particularly in the ghettos. They offer a similar kind of relief to that of heroin. They depress feelings so that you do not have to know how hard it is to be alive. When you come from a ghetto, you are depressed most of the time. Even though you may stagger around with slurred speech and slowed thought processes, it may still feel better than being aware of how unpleasant life can be. Besides, when you are "stoned," you do not notice how poorly coordinated you are.

Reds are readily available in ghettos and relatively easily obtainable by adolescents at all socio-economic levels. They are sold in rolls and can be bought at almost any school in the country, particularly in urban areas. They are addicting and can be very dangerous.

Accidental overdose or suicide can occur, particularly in individuals who take sleeping pills and have developed a tolerance to the sedative effects of the barbiturates. With their sensorium clouded by the drug, not yet to the point of unconsciousness, depressed and sleepless people have continued to take sleeping medications until lethal doses have been ingested. Alcohol, which potentiates the effects of barbiturates, sometimes contributes to this process.

Withdrawal from barbiturates can be extremely dangerous. Even with the most painful withdrawal from heroin, death is not a serious risk. In withdrawing from barbiturates, the body becomes tremulous. As time passes, there is hypotension, fever, vomiting, uncontrolled tremors, and eventually grand mal convulsions, delirium and hypothermia. The probability of grand mal seizures increases with the amount of the drug taken daily. Since withdrawal from barbiturates represents a potentially life-threatening situation, it is essential that this be done under medical supervision. Usually doctors withdraw an individual by decreasing their maintenance levels by approximately ten percent every day or two. Convulsions can occur up to one or even two weeks after sudden withdrawal. This sometimes occurs to individuals in jail who have been separated from their source of drugs. Unfortunately, medically supervised barbiturate withdrawal is rarely, if ever, available in our local jails.

Research has shown that barbiturates change the normal EEG patterns during sleep, reducing the usual amount of rapid eye movement (REM) time. Dreams, which are important in maintaining emotional equilibrium, occur during the REM phase of sleep. Thus, barbiturates may help to create emotional tension. With non-barbiturate sedatives available, perhaps the excessive use and availability of barbiturates will decrease.

Inhalents

Among the very young, children of elementary or junior high school age, there remains the intermittent fads of the inhalation of very toxic substances. These include glues, gasolines, and aerosols. All of them are very dangerous, potentially causing damage to numerous body organs.

Airplane Glue, Plastic and Rubber Cement

When these substances are inhaled initially the effects often are similar to those of early alcohol intoxication, including light-headedness, euphoria, giddiness and exhilaration. Occasionally, vivid colorful hallucinations occur which may last up to 20 to 30 minutes. Other reactions include loss of muscular control, slurred speech, blurred vision, drowsiness, stupor, and gross mental disorientation. In some cases, coma and death have occurred.

The main ingredient in these products is toluene. This organic solvent and others like it are extremely dangerous when repeatedly inhaled. Damage occurs to the brain and central nervous system, as well as to the liver and kidneys. Depression of the blood forming elements in the bone marrow has been reported. Although not addicting, the body rapidly develops a tolerance to toluene. Repeated or regular use of organic solvents can produce severe or permanent damage.

Gasoline, Paint Thinner, Solvents, Kerosene and Lighter Fluid

These hydrocarbons are very toxic, producing distortions similar to that of alcohol intoxication. In addition, ringing or buzzing in the ears and reverberation of sound are common. Prolonged use of these drugs can cause seizures, delirium, hallucinations, coma and in some cases, death.

Aerosol Sprays

Widely used on the American scene, aerosol sprays pour out everything from whipped cream to oven cleaners. They contain propellants which, when inhaled, cause pronounced effects. These usually last only 5 to 10 minutes and include dizziness, uncontrolled laughter and varied hallucinations. Since it is often difficult to separate the propellant from the spray, concomitant inhaling of deodorants or paint often produces long term damage. Freon, when inhaled too rapidly, can freeze the larynx causing edema and death by suffocation.

Asthmador

The belladonna alkaloids can be extremely valuable in pharmaceutical agents, as well as being extremely dangerous or deadly hallucinogenic drugs. Old fashioned asthma preparations, such as asthamador, contain belladonna and in many places are still available over-the-counter. An asthamador trip is usually a tremendously frightening, overwhelming experience. There have been reports of an asthmador trip lasting as much as 7 or 8 days with periods of blindness and extreme confusion.

Conclusion

Those involved in drug rehabilitation are necessarily caught in a double bind. As they represent our society's orthodox view that sees all illegal drugs as "bad," they must present a limited orientation. On the other hand, rehabilitation specialists often realize that they lose the trust of their clients if they take an attitude which morally disapproves of all drugs. It may be difficult to be non-judgmental. Our role as counselors is to help people differentiate between harmful drug abuse and tolerable drug use. The final decision must rest with the individual.

Chapter 8

LANGUAGE OF THE DRUG ABUSER

∽∾∽∾∽∾∽∾∽∾∽∾∽∾∽∾∽∾∽∾∽∾∽∾∽∾∽∾∽∾∽∾∽

Compiled by
RICHARD E. HARDY AND JOHN G. CULL

∽∾∽∾∽∾∽∾∽∾∽∾∽∾∽∾∽∾∽∾∽∾∽∾∽∾∽∾∽∾∽∾∽

THIS SECTION offers a glossary of the language of the drug user. The glossary is in no way complete, but every effort has been made to select those words and terms which may be used most frequently. The reader should remember that the use of these words varies dramatically among geographic regions. A word which is popular in one area may be used very seldom in another.

These words represent the word usage of many addicts throughout the country; however, it is doubtful that any one addict would be familiar with all the included terms.

The argot which addicts use gives a clear description of their way of life. From the terms the reader will be able to discern the compensatory use of drugs by the individual with an inadequate personality and the necessity for many users for escape from reality. Many of the words in the language of the addict are words or modifications used originally by opium smokers, and a number of these words are oriental in origin.

If professionals are to be of help to members of the drug culture they not only must understand the language of the drug abuser but also must have a feeling for the differences in his perceptions of words and his use of language. Work done by the authors (Cull and Hardy, 1973a; Cull and Hardy, 1973b; and

Hardy and Cull, 1973) indicate sub-cultural groups use language in decidedly different fashions. Racial differences and differences in physical capacities cause individuals to use and perceive everyday language in an altered fashion. Consequently, professionals who work with drug abusers must understand the jargon of this group. This glossary is only the first step in developing this understanding.

LANGUAGE OF THE DRUG ABUSER

A

Abe—A five-dollar bill.

Acapulco Gold—A high quality of marijuana.

Acid—LSD (Lysergic Acid Diethylamide). Hallucinogen.

Acid Dropper—One who uses LSD.

Acid Freak—A habitual user of LSD, cube head.

Acid Head—LSD user.

Action—The selling of narcotics. Anything pertaining to criminal activities.

Alcohol—Booze, juice.

Amp.—A 1-cc Methedrine® ampule, legitimate.

Amphetamines—Stimulants which are generally Dexedrine®, Benzedrine®, Methedrine®, or Biphetamine®. Bambita, bennies, bottles, browns, cartwheels, chicken powder, co-pilots, dexies, eye openers, footballs, greenies, hearts, jolly beans, jugs, LA turnabouts, lid proppers, orangies, peaches, pep pills, roses, speed, truck drivers, ups, wake ups, whites.

Amys—Amyl nitrate, stimulant.

Angel Dust—PCP, an animal tranquilizer.

Artillery—Equipment for injecting drugs.

Away—In jail.

Axe—Musical instrument.

B

Back up—A condition in which blood backs up into the syringe while injecting a drug into the vein.

Backtrack—To make sure a needle is in proper position when mainlining by withdrawing the plunger of the syringe before actually injecting the drugs.

Bad Trip—Bummer.

Bag—Situation; category.

Bag—An envelope of heroin (see nickel bag and dime bag).

Bagman—An individual who sells drugs.

Bambita—Desoxyn® or amphetamine derivative.

Bambs—Barbiturates.

Band House—Jail.

Bang—Fix, shot; injection of narcotics.

Barbiturates—Sedatives, usually Seconal®, Nembutal®, Amutal®, Luminal®, Tuinal®, barbs, blue heavens, double trouble, nimbie, peanuts, purple hearts, rainbows, red devils, sleeping pills, yellow jackets.

Barbs—Barbiturates.

Bay State—A standard medical hypodermic syringe, usually made of glass with metal reinforcement, using a plunger and screw-type needle.

Bean Trip—Intoxication from ingesting Benzedrine®; a benny jag.

Beat—To cheat or out bargain.

Bee that stings—A drug habit, especially one coming on; "a monkey on my back."

Belt—The euphoria following an injection of narcotics. A shot, or a quantity of drugs to be injected.

Bennies—Benzedrine®.

Benny Jag—Intoxication from ingesting Benzedrine®.

Bernice—Cocaine.

Bhang—Marijuana. See Cannabis.

Big C—Cocaine.

Big D—LSD.

Big John—The police or any law enforcement officer.

Bindle—A small package of narcotics.

Bit—A prison sentence.

Black and White—A policeman.

Black Beauty—Speed in a black capsule.

Blackjack—Paregoric which has been cooked down to be injected in a concentrated form.

Blank—Bag of non-narcotic powder sold as a regular bag (also dummy, turkey).

Blanks—Gelatin capsules supposedly filled with a drug which are actually filled only with milk powder or sugar powder or sugar cubes supposedly saturated with LSD which have only food color.

Blasted—Under the influence of drugs.

Blast Party—Group gathered to smoke marijuana.

Blotter—A piece of absorbent paper on which LSD has been absorbed.

Blow—To lose something; to smoke marijuana.

Blow a Pill—To smoke opium.

Blow a Stick—To smoke a marijuana cigarette.

Blow Snow—To sniff cocaine.

Blow Weed—To smoke marijuana.

Blue Birds—Blues, barbiturates.

Blue Devil—Amobarbital sodium in solid blue form.

Blue Heavens—Barbiturates.

Blue Mist—A sugar cube colored blue by an LSD preparation.

Blues—Barbiturate.

Blue Velvet—Sodium Amytal®, Pyribenzamine®.

Bombido—Injectible Amphetamine (Also jugs, bottles).

Boost—Steal.

Booster—A professional shoplifter, male or female.

Boot—Pushing and pulling the plunger of a syringe to cause a "rush."

Booze—Alcohol.

Bottles—Injectible amphetamines.

Boy—Heroin.

Bread—Money.

Brick—A kilogram of marijuana compressed under pressure to retain the shape of a brick.

Browns—Long acting amphetamine sulfate (capsules, many colors mainly brown).

Buffotenine—A drug chemically related to DMT derived from dried glandular secretions of certain toads as well as from the *amanita* fungus.

Bum Beef—False complaint or information which usually is given deliberately to the police.

Bum Kick—Boring, unpleasant.

Bum Rap—An arrest or conviction for a crime the man actually did not commit, as distinguished from denying it.

Bum Steer—See bum beef.

Bum Trip or Bummer—A bad trip on LSD.

Bundle—Twenty-five $5 bags of heroin.

Burned—Rendered useless or vulnerable by recognition; e.g., "A narcotic agent was *burned* and unable to continue surveillance." Also, to receive non-narcotic or highly diluted drugs.

Bust or Busted—Arrested; broke.

Buttons—See mescaline.

Buy—A narcotic peddler; a purchase of narcotics.

C

Caballo—Heroin.

Cactus—See peyote.

Cactus Buttons—See mescaline.

Can—A car; A city Jail.

Candy—Barbiturates.

Cannabis—Known variously as Bhang, Charas, Dagga, Ganja, Kit, Macoha, and Marijuana.

Cap—A person, especially a young black, who has to hustle to support his habit. Also, a gelatine capsule or a capsule of drugs.

Cartwheels—Amphetamine sulphate in round, white, double-scored tablets.

Cat Nap—To get small (and very welcome) snatches of sleep during the withdrawal period.

Chalk—Methedrine.

Charas—Marijuana. See Cannabis.
Charged Up—Under the influence of drugs.
Charley—Cocaine.
Charley Coke—A Cocaine addict (restricted to New York and New England).
Chicago Leprosy—Multiple absesses.
Chicken Out—Cop out.
Chicken Powder—Amphetamine powder.
Chip—Heroin.
Chipping—Taking narcotics occasionally.
Chippy—Nice-looking girl.
Chloral Hydrate—Joy juice.
Clear up—To withdraw from drugs.
Clout—To steal, especially as a shoplifter.
Coasting—The sensation of euphoria following the use of a drug. Used of all drugs except cocaine. Serving an easy prison sentence.
Coast-to-Coast—Long-acting amphetamine sulphate in round forms found in many colors. Also LA turnabouts, co-pilots, browns.
Cocaine—Bernice, big c, charley, coke, corine, dust, flake, girl, gold dust, happy dust, heaven dust, her, ice, snow, star dust, white nurse.
Codeine—School boy.
Cohoba—Powdered seeds used as snuff.
Coke—Cocaine.
Coked Up—Under the influence of cocaine.
Cold Turkey—Sudden withdrawal without any alleviating drugs.
Come Down—The end of a trip; the depressed feeling when the drug effects are fading.
Connection—A drug supplier.
Contact—A person who has a connection or who knows a supplier of drugs.
Cooker—Bottle top or spoon used for dissolving Heroin in water over flame.
Cook-It-Up—To prepare heroin (or other opiates) for injection by heating it in a cooking spoon.
Cool(adj.)—In complete control.
Cool(v)—To wait.
Cop a Fix—To obtain a ration of narcotics.
Co-pilots—Amphetamines. Also truck drivers, bennies.
Cop or connect—To buy or get; to purchase drugs.
Cop-out—To inform; to pull out or chicken out; to confess; to alibi.
Cop to—Admit to stealing.
Corine—Cocaine
Cotton—The small wisp of cotton placed in the cooking spoon and used as a filter when the solution is drawn up into the needle.
Cotton Head—A narcotics abuser who depletes his supply of narcotics and attempts to secure one more injection by re-cooking the cotton used from previous fixes.

Crackling Shorts—Breaking into cars.

Crank—Methedrine; stimulant.

Crash—An unpleasant ending of a trip.

Crash Pad—Apartment set up specifically for people to sleep in.

Crib—One's home or apartment. A house of prostitution. A hypochondriac with many persistent symptoms.

Croaker—Unscrupulous doctor who sells drugs or prescriptions to illicit drug users.

Crutch—Device used for holding shortened butt of marijuana cigarette. See roach clip.

Crystal—Methedaine. See speed.

Cube—LSD on sugar cubes.

Cubehead—See acid freak.

Cut—The dilution of a narcotic with substances like lactose (milk sugar) or quinine, strychnine, etc., in order to increase the profit of the drug trafficker.

Cut Out—To leave a certain place.

D

"D"—LSD.

Dagga—See Cannabis.

Daisy—A male homosexual. Also sissy, queen, sex punk.

Dead—No action.

Deal—Sell narcotics to addicts.

Dealer—Anyone who buys or sells stolen goods. A peddler.

Dealing—Keeping on with whatever one is doing; selling dope.

Deck—Several bags of drugs.

Desoxyn®—Amphetamine derivative.

DET—A chemically developed hallucinogenic drug; it has not been found occurring in nature.

Deuce—Two-dollar package of heroin.

Dexies—Dexedrine®, stimulant.

Dig—To understand; to follow.

Dime Bag—A $10 purchase of narcotics.

Dirty—Possessing drugs, liable to arrest.

DMT—A hallucinogen found in the seeds of certain plants native to parts of South America and the West Indies. The powdered seeds have been used for centuries as a snuff "Cohoba."

Dollies—Dolophine®; synthetic opiate equivalent.

Dolly—Methadone.

Dolophine®—Dollies, synthetic heroin.

DOM or STP—(4-Methyl-2, 5-Dimethoxyamphetamine) An hallucinogenic drug produced in the laboratory which induces euphoria and other hallucinogenic effects.

Doo Jee—Heroin.

Dope—Narcotics. Information. To drug. This term, like dope fiend, tends to be taboo among addicts, though they use both perjuratively.

Dope Hop—A prison term for drug addicts, mostly used by guards, turnkeys, and police.

Double Trouble—Amobarbital sodium combined with seconbarbital sodium in red and blue capsules.

Down—Basic; depressed.

Downer Freak—A habitual user of "downers."

Downers—Sedatives, alcohol, tranquilizers and narcotics.

Dragged—A post marijuana state of anxiety.

Drop—Swallow a drug.

Dropped—Taken orally.

Drug—To annoy.

Dry—Without drugs.

Dummy—A bag of non-narcotic powder sold as a regular bag. Also blank, turkey.

Dust—Cocaine.

Dynamite—Something extra special or good.

E

Echos—See flashback.

Eighth—Eighth of an ounce of heroin.

Electric—Overpowering, this is a positive statement.

Eye Dropper—Medicine dropper used with hypodermic needle as makeshift syringe. Most addicts actually prefer it to a syringe.

Eye Opener—Amphetamines.

F

Fag—A pimp. Not to be confused with the general slang fag (a homosexual) clipped from faggot.

Fall—To be arrested. To receive a prison sentence. See bust.

Fat Jay—A Marijuana cigarette approaching the size of a commercial cigarette or larger. They are made large to compensate for weaker types of marijuana.

Fed—A federal agent, usually a narcotic agent. Also, the man, narco.

Finger—Stool pigeon.

Finger Gee—Stool pigeon.

Finger Wave—A rectal examination for contraban narcotics.

Finif or Finski—A $5 bill.

Fink—A stool pigeon; an untrustworthy person. Also wrong, no good, rat.

Five-cent Bag—A $5 heroin fix.

Fix—Injection of narcotics.

Flake—Cocaine.

Flash—A quick jolt of high in abdomen or across chest from heroin shot.

Flashback—Partial reoccurence of an LSD trip.

Flea Powder—Grossly inferior heroin.

Flipped—Becoming psychotic after an overdose of drugs.

Floating—To be high on drugs.

Fly—Sophisticated yet carefree; wise in the ways of the underworld.

Flying—See floating.

Footballs—Amphetamine sulphate in oval-shaped tablets of various colors. Also greenies.

Fox—Good-looking girl.

Freak—An individual who is excessive in some area; for example, "acid freak" or "speed freak."

Freak-out—Bad experience with hallucinogenic drugs.

Fuzz—Policeman or detective.

G

Gal Head—Narcotics addict.

Ganja—Marijuana. See Cannabis.

Garbage—See flea powder.

Gee Stick—An opium pipe. Obsolescent.

George—Very good.

Get a finger wave—The process of having the rectum searched for drugs.

Gig—Job.

Girl—Cocaine.

Give Wings—To start someone else on narcotics.

Going Up—Taking drugs, particularly "uppers."

Gold Dust—Cocaine.

Gold Leaf Special—A Marijuana cigarette which is thought to be very potent.

Goods—Narcotics, especially as they are bought and sold. Used by addicts or dealers in letters, phone calls, or telegrams.

Goof Balls—Barbiturates.

Goofers—See goof balls.

Gow—Narcotics in general, especially those used hypodermically.

Grapes—Wine.

Grass—Marijuana.

Greenies—Amphetamine Sulphate (oval shaped tablets).

Green Score—Profit made by passing counterfeit money.

Gun—Hypodermic needle for injecting Heroin.

H

"H"—Heroin.

Hack—A physician.

Hairy—Heroin.

Hang Tough—Take it easy, quiet down, stop.

Hang Up—A problem, generally a personal problem or a psychological problem.

Happy Dust—Cocaine.

Hard Stuff—Narcotics.

Harpoon—The hollow needle used with a joint. Also spike, silver serpent, pin, machine, tom cat.

Harry—Heroin.

Hashish or Hash—Marijuana.

Hawk—LSD.

Hay—Marijuana.

Head—A user of drugs. Usually a user of LSD.

Hearts—Dextoamphetamine sulphate in orange-colored heart-shaped tablets. Also orangies, dexies, peaches, bennies, roses.

Heat—Police or detective.

Heaven Dust—Cocaine.

Heavy—Deep or profound.

Heeled—See Dirty.

Hemp—Marijuana.

Henry—Heroin.

Her—Cocaine.

Heroin—Boy, caballo, doo jee, "H," Hairy, Harry, Henry, horse, joy powder, junk, scag, scat, skit, smack, stuff, tecata, white lady, white nurse.

High—Under the influence of drugs.

Hip—Aware.

Hippies—Those who like to associate with jazzmen, many of whom are drug users.

Hit—To shoot a narcotic.

Hit On—To ask for.

Hog—PCP.

Holding—See dirty.

Holding—Having drugs in one's possession.

Hooked—Addicted.

Hooker—Hustler, a prostitute.

Hop—Opium for smoking. Narcotics for injection or inhalation.

Hophead—Hype; a drug addict.

Hopped Up—Under the influence of narcotics.

Horse—Heroin.

Hot Shot—Cyanide or other poison concealed in narcotics to kill a troublesome addict.

Hump—To work.

Hustling—Activities involved in obtaining money to buy drugs.

Hype—Drug addict; hophead.

I

Ibogaine—Derived from the roots, bark, stem, and leaves of an African shrub.

Ice—Cocaine.

Ice Cream Habit—See "chipping."

Idiot Juice—Nutmeg and water mixed for intoxication, largely used in prisons.

Indian Hay—Marijuana.

Informer—Stool; an addict assisting police in arresting peddlers.

Iron Horse—A city jail. Most other underworld terms (can, joint, band house, etc.) are also used by addicts.

J

"J"—A joint of marijuana.

Jag—Under the influence of amphetamines.

Jailhouse High—A high obtained from eating nutmeg.

Jeff—To be obsequious, especially Negroes in relation to Whites.

Jive (adj.)—Worthless.

Jive (n)—Marijuana.

Joint—A Marijuana cigarette. The prison.

Jolly Beans—Amphetamines.

Joy Juice—Chloral hydrate.

Joy Pop—Use of heroin in small amounts occasionally.

Joy Powder—Heroin.

Jugs—Injectible amphetamines.

Juice—Alcohol.

Juice Head—An alcoholic.

Junk—Narcotics, usually heroin.

Junker—A Narcotic addict.

Junkie—Narcotic addict.

K

Key—One kilo of marijuana.

Kick—Stop using narcotics through complete withdrawal.

Kick Back—The addicts almost inevitable return to narcotics after having kicked the habit.

Kick Cold—Treatment in which the addict is taken off drugs suddenly.

Kit—See Cannabis.

Kilo—A large amount of narcotics from a pusher's point of view; technically 2.2 pounds. See key.

Knockers—The testicles. A woman's breast.

Knock Out Drops—Chloral hydrate.

L

LA Turnabouts—See coast-to-coast.

Lamb—The passive receptor in a homosexual relationship.

Lame—Square.

Laughing Grass—Marijuana.

Lay Dead—To do nothing.

Lemonade—See flea powder.

Lettuce—Money.

Lid—A small quantity of Marijuana, usually about one ounce.

Lid Proppers—Amphetamines.

Lipton Tea—See mickey finn.

Lit—Under the influence of drugs.

Lit up—Under the influence of drugs.

Load—See "deck."

Loco Weed—Marijuana.

Long-tailed Rat—Stool pigeon.

Louse—A stool pigeon. (Also finger, finger gee, longtailed rat, mouse, rat.)

LSD—Acid, sugar cubes, trips. Lysergic Acid Diethylamide. Big "D." Hawk.

Luminal®—A barbiturate.

M

"M"—Morphine.

Machine—See harpoon.

Macoha—See Cannabis.

MDA—Synthetic stimulant and hallucinogen.

Made—Recognized for what you are.

Main Line (n)—The vein, usually in the crook of the elbow, into which the needle addict injects narcotics.

Main Line (v)—To inject narcotics directly into a vein.

Maintain—Keeping your head during a difficult situation.

Maintaining—Injecting a narcotic directly into a vein.

Mandrix—See Methagualone.

Manicure—Marijuana with everything removed except the leaves.

Marijane—Marijuana.

Marijuana—Bhang, cannabis, charas, ganja, grass, hash, hashish, hay, hemp, Indian Hay, jive, laughing grass, loco weed, marijane, pot, railroad weed, reefer, rope, tea, texas tea, weed.

McCoy—Medicinal drugs in contrast to bootleg drugs.

Medical Hype—A person who has become accidentally addicted during medical treatment for illness or disease; one who obtains bonafide drugs through doctors or hospitals.

Mellowing—The period of a crash when a person is on speed.

Melsedin—(In England) See Methagualone.

MESC—Mescaline; hallucinogenic drug derived from the bottoms of the Peyote cactus plant native to Central America and Southwestern United States. (Also Peyote).

Meth—Methedrine, or methadone.

Methadone—Dolly, Dolophine Amidone®.

Methagualone—An addictive, sedative, hypnotic drug. See Mandrix, Melsedin (In England) Optimil, Parest, Quaalude, "Soapers," Sopor, Straseh-burgh's Taazole (In England).

Mickey—Chloral hydrate.

Mickey Finn or Mickey—Chloral hydrate in a drink to knock out a victim. Also euphemistically, Lipton Tea. A powerful physic such as croton oil, slipped into a whiskey to make the victim sick or to drive him away from a hangout.

Mike—A microgram.

Miss Emma—Morphine.

Mojo—Narcotics of any kind in a contraband trade; but usually morphine, heroin, or cocaine.

Monkey—A drug habit involving physical dependence.

Monkey on my back—Early abstinence symptoms. A drug habit.

Morphine—Hard Stuff, "M," Miss Emma, morpho, white nurse, white stuff, unkie.

Morpho—Morphine.

Mother—An individual's drug peddler.

Mouse—A stool pigeon.

Mr. Twenty-Six—A needle (refers to the gauge of the needle).

N

Nailed—To be arrested.

Narc or Narcos—The law; narcotic agent.

Needle Fiend—An addict who gets pleasure from playing with the needle by inserting an empty needle for the psychological effect.

Needle Freak—One who enjoys using the needle. See needle fiend.

Needle Habit—A habit which is satisfied by hypodermic injections.

Needle Park—To New York addicts, upper Broadway and Sherman Square.

Needle Yen—A desire for narcotics taken hypodermically. A masochistic desire to mainline.

Nembies—Nembutal®.

Nemmies—Nembutal®.

Nickel—A $5 bag of narcotics or marijuana; also a five-year sentence.

Nickel Deck—Five-dollar package of heroin.

Nimbie—Nembutal®.

Nimbies—Nembutal® (pentobarbital).

Nimby—Nembutal® (pentobarbital).

Nod—To be sleepy from a dose of drugs.

Nut City—A mythical place in which anyone feigning insanity is said to live.

O

O.D.—An overdose of narcotics.

Off—Off of drugs, not to be taking drugs at the present time.

Off Someone—To kill someone or to beat someone up.

On Ice—In jail. To lie low or go out of sight temporarily. Wanted by the law.

On the Nod—Sleep from narcotics.

OP—Opium.

Opiates—Narcotics. Generally either opium, morphine or heroin.

Opium—OP.

Optimil—See Methagualone

Orange Owsley—See "Owsley Acid."

Orangies—Dexedrine® (dextroamphetamine, orange colored, heart-shaped tablets).

Out-of-it—Confused, disoriented, unknowing; also, an outside person who is not part of the drug culture.

Out There—Confused.

Overjolt—Overdose of heroin.

Owsley's Acid—LSD (West Coast slang after the illegal manufacturer, Augustus Owsley Stanley, III).

Owsley's Blue Dot—See "Owsley's Acid."

O.Z.—One ounce of marijuana.

P

Pack Heat—To carry a gun.

Pad—User's home; place where he shoots up.

Paid off in gold—Arrested by a federal officer who flashes his gold badge.

Panic—Shortage of narcotics on the market.

Paper—A legal prescription for drugs.

Parest—See Methagualone.

PCP—Angel dust. Peace Pill. Hog.

Peace Pill—PCP.

Peaches—Amphetamine sulphate in rose-colored, heart-shaped tablets. (Also roses, hearts, bennies, orangies).

Peanuts—Barbiturates.

Peddler—A seller of narcotics.

Pep Pills—Amphetamines. Also wake-ups, eye openers.

Pet—The police.

Peter—Chloral hydrate.

Petes—Chloral hydrate.

Peyote—Mescaline.

P.G.—Paregoric.

Phat—Well put together.

Piece—One ounce of heroin; a gun.

Pill Head—Addict on pills.

Pin—See harpoon.

Pink Owsleys—See "Owsley's Acid."

Pinks—Seconal® (seconbarbital sodium).

Pipe—An opium smoker.

Plant—Stash-cache of narcotics.

Pluck—Wine.

P.O.—A parole or probation officer.

P.O.—Paregoric.

Pot—Marijuana.

Pratt or Prat—A hip pocket.

Psilocybin or Psilocyn—Hallucinogenic drugs derived from certain mush-
   rooms generally grown in Mexico.

Purple Hearts—A barbiturate.

Purple Owsley—See "Owsley's Acid."

Pusher—Seller or dealer of drugs.

Put On—To deceive by design; to make fun of or to mislead someone.

Put the bee on—The act of begging narcotics.

Put the croaker on the send—A "fit" or spasm staged by an addict to elicit
   sympathy.

Q

Quaalude—See Methagualone.

Queen—Male homosexual.

Quill—Matchbook cover used to inhale narcotics. Powdered drug is placed
   in fold.

R

Rags—Clothes.

Railroad Weed—Marijuana of poor quality.

Rainbow Roll—An assortment of vari-colored barbiturates, popular among
   addicts on the West Coast.

Rainbows—Amobarbital sodium combined with secobarbital sodium in red
   and blue capsules. Also, red and blues and double trouble.

Rap—Talk.

Rat—Stool pigeon.

R.D.—A red devil.

Red and Blues—See rainbows.

Red Devils—See reds.

Reds—Seconal®; secobarbital sodium.

Reefer—Marijuana cigarette.

Riff—Train of thought.

Right On—Affirmation of a truth; encouragement or support.

Rip Off—Steal or purchase of false narcotics.

Roach—Butt of a marijuana cigarette.

Roach Clip—A device used to hold the butt of a marijuana cigarette.

Rope—Marijuana. So called because when smoked it smells of burning
   hemp.

Roses—Benzedrine® (amphetamine sulphate), rose-colored, heart-shaped tablets.

Rosy—Wine.

Run—Period of addiction.

Rush—The intense orgasm-like euphoria experienced immediately after injecting a drug. Also, flash.

S

Sam—Federal narcotic agents.

Satch—A method of concealing or smuggling drugs into jails.

Satchel—A girl.

Scag—Heroin.

Scat—Heroin.

Scene—Where something is happening.

Schmeck—Heroin.

School Boy—Codeine.

Scortch—To abuse someone verbally and very severely.

Score—To find a source of drugs.

Script—A prescription written by a physician to obtain drugs.

Script Writer—A sympathetic physician; someone who forges prescriptions.

Seccy—Seconal® (secobarbital sodium).

Seconal®—Sleeping pill; depressant, pinks.

Send it home—To inject narcotics intravenously.

Serpent—See harpoon.

Sewer—The vein into which drugs are injected.

Sex Punk—A male homosexual.

Shakedown—To be arrested or held without charges in order to persuade the addict to supply information to police.

Shank—Knife.

Shit—Heroin.

Shoot—See maintaining.

Shooting Gallery—Place where several addicts gather to shoot dope.

Shoot Up—See mainlining.

Short—Car.

Short Go—A small or weak shot.

Shrink—A psychiatrist or psychologist.

Shucking—Wasting time.

Shy—To prepare a pill of opium for smoking.

Silver—See harpoon.

Silver Serpent—See harpoon.

Sissy—A male homosexual.

Sitter—An individual who is sophisticated in the use of drugs, who will oversee others who are on LSD to make sure they don't harm themselves.

Sixteenth Spoon—Sixteenth of an ounce of Heroin.

Skin—Cigarette paper used for a marijuana cigarette.

Skin Popping—Injecting drugs under the skin.

Sleeping Pills—Barbiturates.

Smack—Heroin.

Smashed—High on drugs.

Sneaky Pete—Wine.

Sniff—To sniff narcotics (usually heroin, cocaine, or glue).

Snort—To sniff powdered narcotics.

Snow—Cocaine.

Snowbird—A cocaine user.

Soapers—See Methagualone.

Sopor—See Methagualone.

Sound someone—To feel someone out.

Speed—Methamphetamine; any stimulant, especially, amphetamines.

Speedball—A cocaine-heroin combination.

Speeder—A user of methamphetamine.

Speed Freak—An excessive user of methamphetamine.

Speeding—Using methamphetamine.

Spike—See harpoon.

Splash—Methamphetamine.

Split—To leave a place, sometimes in haste.

Spot Habit—See "ice cream habit."

Square—Lame.

Stable—The community of girls who prostitute for one pimp.

Star Dust—Cocaine.

Stash—A place to hide drugs or money; generally a place well hidden but readily available.

Steam Boat—A tube such as an empty toilet tissue roll which is used to increase the amount of smoke from a marijuana cigarette going into the lungs in order to increase the effectiveness of the cigarette.

Steam Roller—See steam boat.

Stick—A marijuana cigarette.

Stir—Prison.

Stoned—High on drugs.

STP—Hallucinogen; lasts for 72 hours.

Straight—An addict's feeling of well-being after taking drugs.

Strasenburgh's Tuazole (In England)—See Methagualone

Strawberries—An LSD preparation.

Strung-out—Confused.

Stuff—Heroin.

Sugar—Narcotics, generally heroin.

Sugar Cube—This is quite often a vehicle for LSD, a drop of LSD is absorbed by the sugar cube before being taken.

Sunshine—An orange or yellow tablet of LSD reputedly to be of a very potent strength.

Swingman—A drug peddler.

T

T or T Man—A big man. A federal agent, especially a "narco."

Take a Trip—Using LSD.

Take Off—To smoke. To rob a place, especially of narcotics.

Taste—Small quantity of narcotics usually given as a reward or favor.

Tea—Marijuana.

Tea Man—A marijuana user.

Tecata—Heroin.

Ten-cent Pistol—Bag containing poison.

Texas Tea—Marijuana.

THC—Synthetic hallucinogen; produces same effect as marijuana. Tetra hydro cannabinol. The active ingredients in marijuana.

The Man—Policeman or detective.

Ticket—A dose of LSD.

Tie Off—Stopping circulation in order for veins to rise.

Tight—Close.

Tinge—See flash.

Tired—Old or worn out.

Tom Cat—See harpoon.

Tooies—Tuinal® capsules. See double trouble.

Tracks—Scars along the veins after many injections.

Trap—Prison.

Travel Agent—A person who sells LSD.

Trey—Three-dollar bag of narcotics; generally heroin.

Tripping—Taking a hallucinating drug.

Tripping Out—Same as tripping.

Truck Drivers—Amphetamines.

Tuanol®—Sleeping pill; depressant.

Tuinal®—A barbiturate. Also called rainbows or double trouble.

Turkey—Clod or square. A bag of non-narcotic powder sold as a regular bag.

Turn On—To be excited by; to get high on drugs.

TV Action—Euphoria from drugs.

U

Unkie—Morphine.

Uppers—Stimulants; cocaine, speed and psychedelics.

V

Vegetable—A person who has lost all contact with reality due to drugs.

Very Outside—Extremely far out or weird.

Vet—A prison or jail physician.
Vines—Clothes.
Vipe—To smoke marijuana.
Viper—A marijuana smoker.

W

Wake Up—Morning shot.
Wake-ups—Amphetamines.
Wasted—Stoned or drunk.
Way Out—Incomprehensible. The best.
Weed—Marijuana.
Wheels—Car.
White Cross—A white tablet of speed which is sectioned with a cross.
White Lady—Heroin.
White Nurse—A term used to cover cocaine, morphine or heroin; but more
    often morphine.
White Owsley's—See Owsley's acid.
Whites—Amphetamine sulphate in round, white double-scored tablets.
White Stuff—"M," hard stuff, morphine.
Wig—Head, hair.
Wig Out—To become psychotic as a result of narcotics.
Wine—Grapes, pluck, rosy, sneaky pete.
Wired—Addicted on a narcotic drug.
Works—Equipment for injection of drugs.

Y

Yellow Jackets—Nembutal®, barb, depressant. Phenobarbital sodium in
    yellow capsule form.
Yellows—Nembutal®.

Z

Zonked—Under the influence of narcotics.

BIBLIOGRAPHY

Cull, J. G. and Hardy, R. E.: A study of language meaning (gender shap-
    ing) among deaf and hearing subjects. *Journal of Perceptual and Motor
    Skills*, 36, 98, 1973.
Cull, J. G. and Hardy, R. E.: Dissimilarity in word meaning among blind
    and sighted persons, *J Psychol 83*, 333–334, 1973.
Hardy, R. E. and Cull, J. G.: Verbal dissimilarity among black and white
    subjects: a prime concern in counseling and communication. *The Journal
    of Negro Education*, XLII:I, March 1973.

PART II

- COUNSELING THE PARENT OF THE CHRONIC DE-
  LINQUENT
- GUIDED GROUP INTERACTION: A REHABILITATIVE
  APPROACH
- SPECIFIC OBJECTIVES FOR THE INSTITUTIONAL
  TREATMENT OF JUVENILES

Chapter 9

COUNSELING THE PARENT OF THE CHRONIC DELINQUENT

JEROME ROSENBERG

WITH THE GROWTH of our understanding of the factors involved in the development and maintenance of behavioral difficulties, we have come to realize that effective attempts at modification of behavior must now go well beyond the individual who has the specific problems. In this sense we no longer speak about simply a patient or a client, but rather we must place this individual in the context of the environment in which he lives, his family, his society, etc. Consequently, in looking at the problems of behavior of children we have begun to realize that unless we are willing to make the effort to work with the parents and with the school, if the child is of school age, then any effective treatment will be markedly limited. So it is in working in

137

the area of delinquency. Unless we are willing to look into the conditions that produce delinquency, the environment of the home and the interrelationship between the individual delinquent and his parents and all other variables of associations that include this child, we will expend great efforts in treatment with very little positive long-term results.

The model for this chapter will be aimed at the following specifics. First, we will look at the concept of chronic delinquency and procedures for assessing the role of the parents in the particular family situation. Second, we will look at the concept of support intervention in which the major focus of the person involved in working with the family will be to support the parents in adjusting to the particular problems presented by their child. Third, we'll look at a model of change intervention where the focus will be to work with the parents to significantly alter their relationship with their child. Fourth, a dual model in which the focus will be to support the parents in terms of their role in the family situation but also to teach them some basic skills in which they can now work more effectively with their child. Finally, we will summarize and tie the various materials covered together.

Chronic Delinquency and the Role of the Parent

It is obvious by the specific title of this chapter that we are talking about a situation in which the individual delinquent child is a repeat offender to the extent that we can apply the word chronic to describe his overall behavior. Essentially we are saying that whatever attempts have been made to control this behavior in the past have proven to be unsuccessful, and he remains in constant trouble with various authorities in society. In speaking about chronic delinquency we are talking then not about attempts at prevention of delinquent problems, for obviously the problems have been well developed, but we are talking very specifically about an intervention model; an attempt to move into an already existing set of problems and remediate those problems to whatever degree is possible. Our focus here in attempting to remediate is to first understand what is the role between the delinquent in the family, male or female, and the parents. Now here, obviously, the initial assessments to be made by the intervener is the determination of what constitutes the family. This would include whether both parents are living at home, how many siblings, relatives, grandparents, etc., are living within the family constellation. This is important since all of them play an integral part in the maintenance, development, and the hopeful remediation of the problem of the delinquent.

Once we have made this very basic determination, we must then begin to look into the interrelationships between the various members of the family and the delinquent. In doing this, what is required is more than simple interviews with the parents and the delinquent in one's office. What is required here is home visitation, in which the individual who will be working with this child and the parents, will visit the home and spend time in the home observing the interrelationships of behavior within the household. It is very important to carry out this work in the home environment so that there is a chance for concrete changes in behavior under the conditions that those behaviors are most likely to occur. It is clear that any attempts at therapy within a therapist's office is done under the very artificial situations created by an office, in which, the behaviors that occur are often very different from those that are creating the problems in the home environment. Therefore, while information must be gained from the parents in terms of their perception of the home situation and from all other people who have data to bring to the therapist in terms of the home environment, it is critical that direct observations be made, and that they be made more than once so as to guarantee that there is some degree of reliability of the data that has been collected, and some degree of validity concerning what was observed, and that it was not simply created for the benefit of the therapist.

At this point it is important to mention the need for collecting and keeping accurate records concerning specifics of the case on which you are working. Very often records that are tuned to the observations and data collected, particularly on home visitation, can be invaluable in coming up with an effective intervention program that will begin to produce positive changes in the environment in which one is working. In collecting data and in attempting to assess the specifics of the problems, a number of very basic questions must be asked; for how they are answered very often will determine what is the best course of intervention for this particular situation.

The first basic question is concerned with the behaviors that are occurring within this family situation, since the primary concern here is counseling the parents of the delinquent. What then are the behaviors of the parents at this point, in terms of how they relate to and work with their children? Particularly, what are the behavioral patterns of the relationships between the delinquent and his parents or whoever is there within the role of the parents? This means attempting to define as clearly as possible what the interactions are in terms of what does the young child do, how do the parents react to it, how does the child react to them and how does this continuous interaction lead to whatever difficulty may be faced by both parents and the child, at this moment.

In attempting to define the problem, it is also very important to understand just how often the difficulties are occurring. As we look at the particulars of the home situation, we may find that very often it is not so much the specific behavioral interactions that are the problem, but rather the frequency with which they occur. The goal of treatment that is eventually determined for this situation may be not eliminating a behavioral interaction, but reducing how often that behavioral interaction occurs. It is also possible that if it is a good behavior interaction, then treatment will be to increase the frequency with which it occurs.

So we are looking first to define behavioral interactions between the parents and the delinquent, and second, to determine just how often these interactions are occurring. From this, the determination of increasing, maintaining, or reducing these interactions can be made by the person who will be intervening to produce some behavioral changes.

Having defined the behavioral interactions and having gained information on the frequency of occurrences, it is very important to understand what the conditions are in the home environment under which these specific behavioral interactions are occurring. Are there specific situations that lead to specific behaviors or do we find that the interactions between the parent and the child are so pervasive as to defy easy analysis in terms of times of day or what antecedent events may have occurred to lead to this situation. This information is particularly important in terms of helping to focus in on what kind of variables may be occurring; if we could control those variables we might in fact be able to control much of the behavior problem.

To review, the basic questions in defining the behavioral interrelationships between the delinquent and his parents are: (1) What are the behaviors that define the relationships and interactions between parent and child (both good and bad)? (2) What are the frequencies with which their behavior occur? and (3) What are the conditions under which their behavior occur? Now we can go one step further. What kind of variables seem to be maintaining the problem behaviors? Here again we are looking for information that may be available to us and narrow it down so that it leads to some specific prescriptions of treatment. In asking what maintains the behavior, we are concerned with situations in which the parent's reaction to the child serve as a major reinforcer for the child to engage in that same behavior again.

This is particularly true if the child is trying to "bait" the parents; if the parents react as the child expects and desires, one could predict from our knowledge of behavior, that the chances for the child baiting the parents in the future is very high. Therefore, it is the parent's behavior that is maintaining the problem interaction. Again, valuable information to help us define and set up our intervention procedure has been obtained. We can now add the fourth question to our list: (4) What is maintaining the problem behavior?

Having obtained specific data from our observations of the parent and the delinquent's interactions, it is now important to sit down and begin pulling together the picture that has been developed in terms of the environment of the child, particularly the home situation. It is often easy to find obvious problem areas in a home situation, for we know a great deal about the kind of environments that tend to produce delinquency and I think as you look through the various other chapters in this book you will find a wealth of information in understanding many, many variables contributing to delinquent behaviors.

For the purpose of intervening in the home situations and in working with the parents in attempting to develop a means by which they are able not only to find more pleasure in their own lives, but to be more effective in working with the problems created by the chronic delinquent in the family, it is important to focus in on those things that seem to have the highest visibility in terms of problem areas. One factor which is very important in attempting to intervene in any situation is getting some success early in your program. This can go a long way toward winning both the support, the enthusiasm, and the commitment of the parent; not only to continuing the program, but to working more actively to see it succeed. The parents have come to you for help. In that sense at least part of the battle has been won. That is, they recognize the need and they have determined that you are somebody, by virtue of your training who can fill the need.

Now we must also recognize that many parents have come to you by way of the courts, so they may be markedly reluctant to offer any help in whatever you might want to do. This again is part of the data that your observations and interviews with the parents and your home visitation will have given you. And this is part of the assessment you must make to determine what role you will take in working with the parents. You must determine what difficulties you will have in attempting to get the parents to work with you and the best strategy that you could use to go about developing the necessary kind of conditions to allow your intervention to begin. You must then tie this all together, particularly the definition of the problem, the frequency of the occurrence of the problem, the conditions under which it occurs and what you have determined seems to be maintaining this behavior, so that you can be comfortable in your position as the help agent. Now you are in a position to make some determination as to what your strategy will be.

This leads us to the next three areas.

1 SUPPORT INTERVENTION—First, the parent is functioning at a very high level of efficiency and it would appear that all their best efforts; efforts that you would support, are not working. Consequently, the parents do not need to be taught new techniques but rather need to be given the necessary support to allow them

to continue to do the work they are doing, allow them to find something within this situation that is positive for them to work with and to help them through the continuous crises situation that are defined by the chronicity of the delinquency problem.

2 CHANGE INTERVENTION—The second alternative is that your assessment of the family situation has determined that the parents are basically ineffective in what they are doing and they need to be taught specific techniques that will allow them to effectively work with their child. Here your role will be partially an educator and partially a therapist because your ultimate focus is to get them to be more effective at how they work with their child. The amount of time available for you to work with the parents or the child is markedly limited, but if you are successful with the parents they have their whole future to work with this youth.

3 SUPPORT-CHANGE COMBINATION—The third option left open to you; based upon your initial assessment of the family situation, is that the parent not only needs to have basic techniques taught to them but they have tried very hard and need a great deal of support to continue the efforts and support for them to make the attempt to learn a new approach and to carry it out. This can be seen as a combination program of both support for the parent and teaching them to use new techniques to handle the old chronic problems that they have been having to face.

I. Support Intervention

In situations where the delinquency problem is a chronic one, it would seem obvious that the amount of energy, the investment of time, and the amount of stress that the parents have been through will have been both long in duration and high in frequency. Consequently, it is very likely that the parents of the chronic delinquent will be very close to that point in which they will not only be markedly inefficient in how well they work with the delinquent, but at the point in which giving up (condemning themselves as losers and as poor parents) is very close if not already reached. Therefore, probably in all programs of intervention and working with the parent of the chronic delinquent, it will be necessary for some supportive role to be played by the therapist.

Total intervention on the part of the therapist is best handled by a straight, total supporter role, and would be based upon an assessment of the situation in which the efforts of the parents have been good efforts. The programs that they have worked with have under the circumstances, been good programs. The parents have not lacked for an involvement with the child, but as is true in so many of our delinquency cases today, delinquency is unexpected, based on looking into the home in which there tends to be many, many positive factors that simply would not be predictive of delinquency. Therefore, this parent needs a great deal of supportive counseling on the part of the therapist; part hand-holding and part recognition that they deserve to be reinforced for their continuous efforts to this point.

It is also important to help them understand and assess honestly their role in the problem so they do not feel a stronger sense of guilt than may be appropriate for the situation. It is important that they understand that all their efforts, however inefficient and however difficult they may have seemed in the past, probably have maintained the situation so that it has not gotten any worse than it is. They should also understand that their commitment as parents is being met at the highest level and there are many circumstances in which the love, faith, and the help of the parent simply have proven to be not enough to control certain behaviors that develop under influences that the parents simply do not have enough control over. By proving these things to the parents it will help them continue to see themselves in a positive role in working with their child.

Also, the therapist's supportive role will be in terms of the kind of things the parents want to continue doing. They should feel free to talk with the therapist concerning changes in their attitude that they think might be affective in working with their child. And again, the likelihood that the parents will find themselves continually involved with various authorities, police, courts and probation officers, they will need somebody not only to support them in their continuous on-going crisis situation, in the chronic aspects of never knowing what will happen next, and in the constant pressure of meeting demands placed on them by the courts and others; the support of somebody who can convey to them necessary information to understand the judicial system, the court system, and the police role will also be needed.

I think that in working with many parents you find ignorance of what is happening contributes to much of the real stress. When the parents are well-informed of what is happening however, they may have no control over the situation, but they are much more capable of coping with their own needs as well as those of the chronic delinquent.

The frequency of contacts of the supportive program should be determined by the initial assessment. If the parents are at a critical point in their involvement and need to be seen very frequently, then I think visitation should be done as often as possible. Again, crisis intervention becomes a very critical kind of thing, and support is being available—whether it is a call or a visit in the middle of the night. Sometimes, just being available is one of the strongest supports a parent can have, because they always know that there is somebody who cares, somebody who is willing to listen and somebody who is willing to put out an extra effort to help them.

As determined by the initial assessment, additional supportive measures will be determined by the degree of the problem, by how long it has been going on, by what immediate factors are present in the situation and what long term factors need to be considered. Probably one visit a week on the average would be sufficient for most situations. Many visits could be every two weeks, some once a month, and some even longer than that. Other cases may need to be seen two, three times a week or some even more.

It is clear that with the development of crisis intervention centers throughout the country a twenty-four hour a day phone line can be invaluable in handling immediate crisis situations that come up at times in which agencies are usually unavailable. If there is a crisis intervention program available in your community the parents should be made aware of it. If no such program is available, then you as the therapist probably should be available when necessary on twenty-four hour call. What is important is that the parents in need have somebody to support them, to be there to back them up when problems occur and to know that they can count on you. And in that sense, just being there can mean a great deal of difference in how well they are able to handle not only the day-to-day problems that they must face, but those constant crisis situations that all too often will be sprinkled in with the continuous chronic problems created by the delinquent situation.

It is important to recognize that while some distinction is being made between kinds of intervention, it is highly possible for one particular intervention technique to move into another, as conditions in the situation change and as you are able to gain more information and knowledge of the interrelationship between the parents and the delinquent youth. It is important to recognize that how you do the specific interventions of the supportive program are determined by your viewpoint on therapy, but even more critically, by the data you collected in assessing what the problem was. Therefore, to give you a rote supportive model is to do an injustice to the data you collect and the need for you to be responsive to the problem as observed and defined by you during the course of your early interviews and home visitation.

Again, recognizing the need to be responsive to your data and to the changes in your observation, it is highly likely that movement from a supportive model to a change intervention model can occur at any time; depending upon the specific behaviors of the chronic delinquent in the family and the changing environmental conditions that occur because of the delinquent's behavior. Consequently, let us now look at the change intervention model.

II. Change Intervention

With the major focus of the intervention model being to change the manner in which the parents themselves behave as it relates to the delinquent in the family, there are two methods that can be used to bring about this change. The choice is dependent in part upon the kind of relationship that has been established between you as a therapist and the parents over the period of time you have been working with them.

The first method would be based upon a well-developed mutual trust so that you can clearly show the parents what they are doing and that at the moment is not being effective in helping the child. You can give them a strong awareness of their current behavior and begin developing in them an appreciation for alternative patterns of behavior that they might use as it relates to specific examples that you are able to demonstrate. Here it is very critical that you offer the parent something that they can point to, acknowledge and begin to use as a means of measuring the degree of change they are able to accomplish.

The second particular model is based upon a situation in which the relationship between the therapist and the family has not developed well or is a new one. The data indicates that drastic changes must be accomplished quickly in the parents' behavior in order to mitigate some of the problems developing in the family and also to give the parents a much more effective role in attempting to work with the delinquent. Here it would take a much more directive approach in determining what problem behaviors need to be worked through. The therapist would go directly to those behaviors, discuss them with the parents and offer very specific suggestions as to what changes should be made. In essence, the therapist would be programming the parents to engage in those behaviors deemed necessary to effectively change the relationship between the delinquent and the family. This would be based upon the data that identifies the specific situations in which behavioral interactions lead to very negative kind of repercussions for both members of the family.

Any number of models can be used in working with the parents, from specific role playing techniques to give them the necessary verbal and non-verbal behavior, to the use of a basic shaping procedure on the part of the therapist for the parent's behavior. Here, the specific goal is to allow the parents to create a much greater impact in terms of the on-going family situation and to allow them to exercise all the powerful controls available to them as parents in a significantly more affective and meaningful way than they have apparently been doing in the past.

Here, as in the other situation, the more quickly you can show a successful change in behavior the stronger your position will be in helping the parents to continue to change in the necessary direction. Therefore, in a selection of any of the parents' behavior that you want to change as it relates to the delinquent in the family, the problem selected should be a simple one, a very obvious one, and one that from your professional judgment, will show the greatest degree of change with the suggestions that you are going to institute in the parent-child relationship. One must be cautioned not to select a problem area that will be so long term in treatment and so difficult to change that the degree of frustration that sets in will far exceed the ability to succeed. If necessary the parents and child are to begin to change their own behavior and in this case in the direction of more positive interrelationship.

Other than a recognition, there are a variety of techniques that exist in the field of behavior change, ranging from non-directive therapy to very directive varieties of behavior-modification and behavior therapy. The treatment of choice should be determined by the therapist in conjunction with the family based upon the observations and data collection used in assessing the initial problem.

The literature listed in the bibliography at the end of this chapter make available to the practitioner a wide range of resources and variety of treatment techniques that can be identified and adopted.

The critical issue for the practitioner to be aware of is the variety of treatment programs that exist in the literature far exceed the general range of problems you are likely to encounter in any given situation. What is most critical is the preliminary steps in which an assessment of the particular problem allows you to select the treatment of choice. In the case of working with parents of chronic delinquents, the situations are very similar to any home environment in which the parents find themselves in a position of very little meaningful behavior control, particularly as it relates to the problem child. In this sense, a generalized home management program can be developed, keyed to the range of problems presented by the delinquent in the family putting us in a position to effectively bring about some changes both in the behavior of the delinquent and in the behavior of the parents.

With this concept of the change intervention model, we can now recognize that in many cases two factors will be operating. First is the need to support the parents through their serious trials and tribulations and secondly to significantly alter the behavior of the parent so that they become more effective in working with their delinquent child. Consequently, a combination treatment-support model would use both programs previously discussed.

III. Combination Support-Change Intervention

The sequence in ordering the intervention would include support first. When this has become an effective intervention then change in the behavior of the parent would come next. Support would never be discontinued, but the focus would move from support to behavior change. The degree to which the parents effectively are able to change their behavior and consequently effectively change the behavior of their delinquent child, will determine the need for support. It is expected it will become somewhat less, because the parents will begin to have successes that they themselves can look to and allow themselves a good degree of self-reinforcement and self-support.

Ultimately, the goal of any intervention with the child and with the parents is to give the necessary maintenance and controls of that behavior to those who must exist in the situation. Therefore, the degree to which the parents can begin to become self-supportive, capable of determining the situation and the appropriate behaviors for their situation on their own, is where the therapist has been singly effective in carrying out their role in altering the problem.

Just as the therapist must determine and assess the nature of the behavior problem, this is also something that the parent must be taught by the therapist to allow them to more fully appreciate what is happening within the situation that is producing the greatest degree of stress, and to allow them to focus on those areas with the most meaningful attempts at behavior change.

To summarize, there are a number of basic steps necessary for a practioner to follow to be most effective in working with the parents of chronic delinquent youths. First, is a critical need to observe and assess the nature of the parent-child interactions. This includes not only interviews and observations of the parent in the office but through home visitations and discussions with those who have input into the family situation so that a comprehensive picture can be developed of what conditions are and how things exist in the day-to-day life of the parent and the delinquent youth.

Second; based upon these observations, the practioner must decide what mode of therapy is most desirable. First, we discussed a supportive type, in which the stress on the parents is shared to some degree by the therapist to allow them to function more capably under the conditions that exist, to allow them to have access to a resource on a continual basis in helping them understand the nature of the situation and to feel free to call on somebody when questions come up or when they feel that they are in some kind of crisis situation.

We have pointed out that in a chronic delinquency situation the frequency of the problems are going to be very high, the duration of the stress situations are going to be quite long and a supportive role on the part of the therapist becomes critically important.

We talked about a change intervention role in which the therapist determines from his observations of the problem that the parents are themselves functioning ineffectively and very basic behavior changes are necessary on their part for them to begin to have a positive interaction with the delinquent. The parents are shown, either through directed changes in their behavior, through a process of shaping their behavior, or through a combination of insight and alternative presentations of behavior, what they can now do to change the relationship between them and the delinquent. Here the stress is on selecting a problem area that has a high likelihood of successful change, so that the parents of the child can taste success early rather than continually building up another frustration that has become part of the chronicity of the problem.

Finally, we talked about a combination role in which the therapist would find himself both giving support; particularly during the early stages of the relationship with the family, and then initiating a combination support-behavior change model in which work with the parent would be to find alternative behaviors to the ones they are using, while at the same time giving them strong support for the crisis situations that occur. The focus and goal of all the situations are to allow the parent to become self-supportive, to allow them to become able to modify and adjust their own behavior to handle situations, and to produce a significant change within the complex of the family situation as it relates to the parents and the delinquent child.

In closing, let me again reiterate that techniques for behavior change are available in a variety of journals and in a variety of books which are cited at the end of this chapter. What is often missing is the ability to determine what is the treatment of choice for the given problem that one is facing. With the recognition of the need to work in the home if we are to effectively change the behavior of the problem child, we should realize that in working in the home we are talking specifically about working with the parents. A necessary factor in working in a situation where the problem is chronic delinquency is to assess through observation and data collection what are the problems that the parents themselves have and what the problems are as the parents relate to the delinquent child. From this gathering of data and assessment of the situation, one is in a better position to determine what is the treatment of choice and what intervention should be done. It would be expected that the degree of successful outcome is far better for this kind of preparation than it would be if one were to simply get involved in a situation without determining what all the variables were that were part of the relationship between the parents and the chronic delinquent.

One additional note that can be very helpful for all concerned. Clarification of the roles and responsibilities of the parents and the therapist are very important. In order to measure the degree of accountability assumed by all concerned, a contract between the therapist and the family in which all the particulars are spelled out can be a very valuable tool for treatment and determining the degree of success. This should be entered and modified as the therapist's involvement with the parents changes. It will serve as an excellent guideline for the behavior of all concerned.

BIBLIOGRAPHY

Aldrich, C. K.: Thief. *Psychol Today,* 4:10, 1971.

Bailey, Jon S., Wolf, M. M., and Philips, E. L.: Home-based reinforcement and the modification of pre-delinquent's classroom behavior. *J Appl Behav Anal,* 3:5, 1970.

Bandura, A.: *Principles of Behavior Modification.* New York, Holt, Rinehart, and Winston, 1969.

Becher, W. C.: *Parents are Teachers: A Child Management Program.* Research Press, 1971.

Bijou, S. W. and Baer, D. M.: *Child Development: Readings in Environmental Analysis.* New York, Appleton, 1967.

Burchard J., and Tyler, V., Jr.: The modification of delinquent behavior through operant conditioning. *Behav Res Ther,* 2:245–250, 1965.

Coe, W. C.: *A Family Operant Program.* Paper Presented at Western Psychological Association, Los Angeles, 1970.

Deibert, A. N., and Harmon, A. V.: *New Tools For Changing Behavior.* Research Press, 1970.

Engela, R., Kawtson, J., Laughy, L., and Garlington, W.: Behavior modification techniques applied to a family unit—a case study, *J Child Psychol Psychiatry,* 9:245–252, 1968.

Guerney, B. F., Jr. (Ed.): *Psychotherapeutic Agents: New Roles For Non-Professionals, Parents, and Teachers.* New York, Holt, Rinehart, and Winston, Inc., 1969.

Hall, R. U.: *Managing Behavior.* Part I Behavior Modification—The Measurement of Behavior; Part II Behavior Modification—Basic Principles; Part III Behavior Modification-Application In School and Home. *H & E Enterprises,* Inc., 1970.

Hawkins, R. P., Peterson, R. F., Schevard, Edda, and Byere, S. W.: Behavior therapy in the home: Amelioration of problem parent-child relations with the parent in a therapeutic role. *J Exp Child Psychol* 4:99–107, 1966.

Holland, C. J.: An interview guide for behavioral counseling with parents. *Behav Ther* 1:70–79, 1970.

Johnson, James M.: *Using Parents As Contingency Managers.* Paper Presented at Eastern Psychological Association, 1969.

Johnson, S. M., and Brown, R. A.: Producing behavior change in parents of disturbed children. *J Child Psychol Psychiatry, 10:*107–121, 1969.

Krumboltz, J. D., and Thoresen, C. E.: *Behavioral Counseling: Cases and Techniques.* New York, Holt, Rinehart, and Winston, 1969.

McIntire, R. W.: *For Love of Children: Behavioral Psychology For Parents.* Del Mar, Calif., C. R. M. Books, 1970.

McIntire, Roger W.: Spare the rod, use behavior mod. *Psychol Today, 4:*1, 1970.

Mira, M.: Results of a behavior modification training program for parents and teachers. *Behav Res Ther, 8:*309–311, 1970.

Patterson, G. R. and Ebner, M. J.: *Applications of Learning Principle to the Treatment of Deviant Children.* American Psychological Association Convention, Chicago, 1965.

Patterson, G. R. and Fagot, B. I.: Selective responsiveness to social reinforcers and deviant behavior in children. *Psychol Record, 17:*369–378, 1967.

Patterson, G. R., Littman, R. E., and Hinsey, W. C.: Parental effectiveness as reinforcers in the laboratory and its relation to child rearing practices and child adjustment in the classroom. *J Pers, 32:*180–199, 1964.

Peine, H. A.: *Programming the Home.* Paper Presented to Rocky Mountain Psychological Association, 1969.

Ray, R. S.: *Parents and Teachers as Therapeutic Agents in Behavior Modification.* Paper Presented to Second Annual Alabama Behavior Modification Institute, 1969.

Rickard, H. C. (Ed.): *Behavioral Intervention in Human Problems.* Elmsford, N. Y., Pergamon, 1972.

Schwitzgebel, R. L.: Short-term operant conditioning of adolescent offenders on socially relevant variables. *J Abnorm Psychol, 72:*137–142, 1967.

Shala, S. A.: *Training and Utilizing a Mother as a Therapist For her Child.* Paper Presented to Eastern Psychological Association, 1967.

Stuart, R. B.: *Behavioral Contracting Within the Families of Delinquents.* Paper Presented at American Psychological Association, 1970.

Tharp, R. G., and Wetzel, R. J.: *Behavior Modification in the Natural Environment.* New York Acad Pr, 1969.

Thorne, G., Tharp, R., and Wetzel, R.: Behavior modification techniques: new tools for probation officers. *Fed Probation* (March, 1967).

Terdal, L. and Buell, J.: Parent education in managing retarded children with behavior deficits and inappropriate behaviors. *Ment Retard, 7:* no. 3, 10–13, 1969.

Tighe, T. J., and Elliott, R.: A technique for controlling behavior in natural life settings. *J Appl Behav Anal, 1:* no. 3, 263–266, 1968.

Ulrich, R., Stachaik, T., and Mabry, J.: *Control of Human Behavior: From Cure to Prevention.* Glenview, Ill. Scott F 1970.

Wagner, M. K.: Parent therapists: an operant conditioning method. *Ment Hyg*, 52:452–455, 1968.

Walder, L. O., Cohen, S. J., Breiter, D. W., Warman, F. C., Orme-Johnson, D. and Pauey, S.: Parents As Change Agents. In S. E. Golann and C. Eisdorfer (Eds.): *Handbook of Community Psychology.* New York, Appleton, 1971.

Wahler, R. G., Winkel, G., Peterson, R., and Morrison, D.: Mothers as behavior therapists for their own children. *Behav Res Ther*, 3:113–124, 1965.

Chapter 10

GUIDED GROUP INTERACTION: A REHABILITATIVE APPROACH

James O. Finckenauer

ᔑᔑᔑᔑᔑᔑᔑᔑᔑᔑᔑᔑᔑᔑᔑᔑᔑᔑᔑᔑᔑᔑᔑᔑᔑᔑᔑ

ᔑᔑᔑᔑᔑᔑᔑᔑᔑᔑᔑᔑᔑᔑᔑᔑᔑᔑᔑᔑᔑᔑᔑᔑᔑᔑᔑ

THE RESIDENTIAL GROUP centers in New Jersey have represented a unique project in using a group approach in the treatment of juvenile delinquency. Histories of the evolution of the "Highfields" program, including descriptions and careful evaluations, have been presented elsewhere and need not be replicated here. However, the core of the program; the guided group interaction sessions which represent the key to success in any effort to duplicate the Highfields concept, need to be re-examined in greater detail for the benefit of those practitioners attempting to implement guided group interaction. Such implementation is now beginning or ongoing in juvenile correctional institutions, residential and nonresidential community-based rehabilitation facilities, junior high and high schools, police department juvenile aid bureaus, etc; and it is being used with committed adolescent offenders, parolees, school dropouts, boys, girls, school problem children, probationers and unemployed youths.

Guided group interaction has been defined as the use of free discussion in a friendly supportive atmosphere to re-educate delinquents to accept the restrictions of society by finding greater personal satisfaction in conforming to social rules than in following delinquent patterns. It attempts to aid group members by developing understanding of their current problems through interaction with others. The subjects discussed in the guided group revolve around current problems of group members and of the group itself. These problems emerge as a result of interaction with significant others, primarily peers, and in the group meetings themselves are crucial to guided group interaction.

The guided group sessions serve as a means for stabilizing the lives of adolescents, and as a medium through which each young person is able to come to grips with his or her problems. The major emphasis in this technique is on the group and its development, rather than upon an exhaustive analysis of each group member. Thus, the method is only somewhat similar to group therapy. Unlike formal group therapy, the group leader need not be a clinician. More important than any formal academic training are a perceptive understanding of adolescents and their problems, particularly the influence of peer pressures upon behavior; an empathic ability to establish rapport with the members of the particular group without being threatening or threatened; and an understanding of the group process in changing human behavior.

Guided group interaction is considered to be most effective with adolescents because they are perhaps more responsive to peer influences than any other particular age group. Because participation in the group process requires an intellectual understanding of the complexities and subtleties of that process, it is not desirable to include as group participants any young people who are mentally retarded to an extent that would not permit them to function intellectually in the program.

Persons with severe psychological disorders (advanced neuroses or psychoses) also should be excluded for several important reasons:

1. The group pressures can be extremely threatening and damaging to an individual psychologically incapable of handling them.
2. The group leader in all likelihood does not possess the necessary psychological or psychiatric training to deal with severe mental or emotional disorders.
3. The group members who are the most important change agents will neither understand nor be able to cope with mentally or emotionally disordered individuals.

Eight to twelve members are considered to be the optimum size for guided group; and three to five meetings per week of one to two hours duration have proven to be most productive. Each group within the Highfields concept proceeds through a series of stages in its development from an aggregate of approximately ten strangers to a closely knit primary group whose members are able to relate to one another in some significant way.

In the formative beginning of a group, there is little or no discernible group structure. The members engage in seeking information about one another, the group leader, and their environment; in testing the situation by engaging in hostile, defensive behavior, and by paying lip service to conventional standards.

The second stage is characterized by the development of an awareness of themselves and others, as well as the formation of cliques within the larger group. A clique is a subgroup of the total group. It is a defensive measure designed to protect the persons in the clique from the remainder of the group, including the group leader. Through mutually supportive interaction in the group sessions, the members of the clique can pretend to change their deviant behavior while actually avoiding such change. This is what is commonly known as "beating the program."

The cliques must be analyzed, discussed and broken by the total group before frank, honest and open discussion and resolution of all the problems of all the group members can occur. Deviant social roles and self-conceptions are revealed at this time, and a great deal of tension is generated around revealing one's feelings about other members.

The third stage is the critical period. The clique ties are broken and identification with the larger group is demanded.

The sessions are characterized by an expression of intense hostility, particularly toward the group leader; defenses are breached and much frustration is experienced. The outcome of this struggle is a high degree of group solidarity and mutual identification. Also involved in this process is the idea of reforming one's self by attempting to reform others. The group member accepts the common purpose of the group, identifies himself closely with other persons engaged in reformation, and assigns status to others on the basis of conventional behavior.

The final stage is a relatively short period of intense, constructive activity. There is a direct assault on each member's problems, and an expression in action of confidence in the group's ability to resolve any difficulty. There is a minimal dependence on the group leader. The members review each other's roles, interpersonal relationships, and past and present behavior.

AN EVALUATION OF THE IMPACT OF GUIDED GROUP INTERACTION

An evaluative look at the impact of guided group interaction was obtained several years ago when I conducted a simple research study of 50 boys in the three New Jersey residential group centers who were narcotics users. Narcotics users, as opposed to addicts, generally use drugs primarily as a means of sharing a social activity with others. Users generally do not become physiologically dependent upon drugs nor find it necessary to increase the dosage because their usage is a social activity, the initial goal of which is socialization rather than getting high. Some of these 50 boys had been admitted for using narcotics while others were admitted for other offenses, but also had a history of drug use. Although none of the boys were "hard core" drug addicts, a number of them had regularly experimented with heroin. The primary hypothesis being tested was that if the genesis of narcotics use among juveniles is largely a socialization process, then the residential group center program utilizing guided group interaction should be successful in its treatment of the juvenile drug user, since the orientation of guided group interaction is resocialization.

The post-release adjustment reports of the narcotic users were analyzed in order to determine the boys' status and the quality of their adjustment in the community a minimum of six months after leaving the centers.

From the original sample of 50 boys, reports were available on 38 boys, five did not complete the program successfully, i.e. they were classified as unsuitable and either ran away or were returned to juvenile court. The remaining seven had not been in the community for the minimum period of six months necessary to assess their adjustment. The findings are shown in Table 10–I.

The table shows that 76.5 percent of the users could be termed successes. Of these, 37 percent, or better than one in three, made good adjustments. Although 23.5 percent committed new offenses, only 13 percent were considered serious enough to warrant commitment to the reformatory. Thus, 87 percent, with varying degree of adjustment, were still in the free community.

TABLE 10–I
POST-RELEASE ADJUSTMENT OF NARCOTIC USERS

Adjustment	Number	Per Cent
Good	14	37
Average	15	39.5
Poor (New Offenses)	4	10.5
Very Poor (Committed to the reformatory)	5	13
Total	38	100

If the five boys classified as unsuitable for the Highfields program were included in the figures in Table 10–I the results still indicated a favorable success rate by a comfortable margin. As shown in Table 10–II 67.5 percent were successes, and 81.5 percent were in the community.

TABLE 10–II
POST-RELEASE ADJUSTMENT OF NARCOTIC USERS
INCLUDING UNSUITABLES

Adjustment	Number	Per Cent
Good	14	32.5
Average	15	35
Poor (New Offenses)	6	14
Very Poor (Committed to the reformatory)	8	18.5
Total	43	100

These figures reflect favorably upon the success of the residential group center program, and particularly guided group interaction, in its treatment of the juvenile narcotic user. Conceding the fact that the program was dealing with users rather than addicts, the results must still be impressive. Further, it is felt that these figures would be impressive when compared with those from any program dealing with narcotic users, juvenile or adult.

GROUP SIX—A CASE STUDY

In order to illustrate the foregoing overview, I wish to draw upon my own initial experience as assistant superintendent at New Jersey's Ocean Residential Group Center, for which Highfields was a prototype. One of my responsibilities was to conduct guided group interaction sessions. The description and assessment of the group which follows was my first experience with this technique.

Group Six came into existence as a group in July. The oldest members, in reference to length of stay, had arrived during the latter part of June. These and all other arrivals prior to the end of July were overlapping members in the previous group. In all, there were nine such overlapping members. Four boys arrived during the first week of August to give the group a total membership of thirteen. However, one boy ran away and was returned to juvenile court after one day in residence; and two other boys ran away after several weeks in residence, committed new offenses, and were subsequently sent to the reformatory. The fourth boy was returned to court as unsuitable, and he too was sent to the reformatory. Thus, the final size of Group Six was nine members.

HARRY: The first boy in the group, Harry, was seventeen years old. He was the oldest boy in reference to length of stay in the program. He had first been known to the juvenile court at the age of twelve when he was arrested for larceny and attempted breaking and entry. At this time, he was placed on probation for one year. He was dismissed from probation with improvement the following year.

At age fourteen he was again arrested on two counts of breaking and entry, larceny, and multiple shoplifting. He was given a suspended sentence to the State Home for Boys and placed on probation for three years. Two years later he was again apprehended for shoplifting and his probation was continued. The following year he was discharged from probation with improvement.

At seventeen he was arrested and charged with three counts of breaking, entry, and larceny and breaking and entry. For these offenses he was given a suspended sentence to the Annandale Reformatory for Males and placed on probation for one year with the condition that he attend the Highfields program.

Harry was Catholic, had three sisters, and his father was alcoholic. He had a poor school record and was a flagrant truant. His I.Q. tested at 97. He was characterized as being helpful at home, respectful of authority, but as having poor self-control.

BILL: The second oldest boy in the group, Bill was a somewhat weak and immature boy of eighteen. He had first appeared in court the previous year for possessing and drinking alcoholic beverages. In addition, he had committed numerous motor vehicle violations. Bill had been without a father for ten years and was not properly supervised by his mother who was employed on a full-time basis as the owner of a tavern. He had developed a serious drinking problem at a very young age.

Bill was ordered to the State Diagnostic Center at Menlo Park where his condition was diagnosed as "maladjustment reaction of adolescence with dissocial traits." The prognosis was good, but it was recommended that his needs for control, guidance and goals be met immediately. It was felt that he had to be shown "that he cannot get away with dictating his terms to the world around him, whether it be through ingratiation or through threats."

EDDIE: Eddie was a seventeen-year-old narcotics user from an upper middle class family consisting of his mother and stepfather. He had previously been placed on unofficial supervision with improvement.

When last apprehended for larceny of doctors' bags, Eddie admitted consuming such forms of barbiturates as Seconal®, Miltown®, Tuninal®, and Nembutal® over a period of two and a half years. For a period of six months, he also injected himself with heroin, morphine, Demerol®, morphine acetate and cocaine.

This boy possessed above average intelligence (I.Q. 121), and came from a good home. His probation officer characterized him in the following manner: "He lacks initiative, is irresponsible, and is content 'floating through life,' being a crutch on his parents in particular, and society in general."

ART: The fourth oldest boy in the group, Art was seventeen. He lived with his mother and stepfather who was an attorney. He had been apprehended on numerous occasions for motor vehicle larceny and driving without a license.

His commitment to the New Jersey State Diagnostic Center at Menlo Park resulted in the following report:

"*Diagnosis:* Personality Trait Disturbance, Emotional Immaturity.

Prognosis: In the present day setting he has missed too much school and possibly still has some reading disability to be able to pursue any career which would require some scholastic achievement. Pushing him in this direction will create further difficulties. Being volatile emotionally and immature he will be subjected to the influences of others and a similar act may be repeated. He, however, does not seem to be antisocial and aggressive.

Recommendation: . . . . The staff believed that at the present time probationary measures, referral to a Mental Hygiene Clinic and training in some trade such as auto mechanic while on probation is indicated. A provision to have him in a correctional institution should the offense be repeated, is recommended as a deterrent."

MIKE: Mike, a sixteen-year-old-boy, was admitted into the Highfields program for motor vehicle larceny and drunken disorderly conduct. He had first appeared in court the year before for possession of a stolen car, at which time he was adjudged delinquent and placed on probation.

Mike later appeared in juvenile court for drunkenness and on charges of trespassing on property, continual annoyance of family, and breaking, entry and larceny. He had dropped out of school after having an extremely poor attendance record and being considered a behavior problem in school.

Much of Mike's problem was considered to be his father's drinking and extremely neurotic behavior. Because of this and his mother's outside employment, family control was limited.

Most of his difficulties in the community occurred while he was involved in group activity. He was extremely desirous of peer group acceptance and would go to some lengths to attain it. He seemed to have little ability to be alone or direct himself.

CRAIG: Craig came from a family in which his siblings had a history of delinquency. The probation department felt that he was a follower who was easily mislead into deviant behavior, and that he had little insight or control in regard to himself. Also, it was felt that his difficulties stemmed partly from a parental lack of concern and the fact that he was free to roam the streets and do as he pleased. Craig's previous history of delinquency indicated the offenses of breaking, entry, entry and larceny, disorderly, possession of alcohol, disorderly, consumption of alcoholic beverages, and escaping from the police headquarters

Craig was a fairly quiet but tough "farm boy" type from a rural area. His delinquency was of a relatively unsophisticated but aggressive nature. The fact that he was relatively short, although muscular, and had previously lost one eye might indicate that his aggressiveness was partially compensatory.

PETE: Pete, age sixteen, first appeared in court on charges of larceny the previous year. He was later charged with sniffing glue, an offense which was committed numerous times. Members of his peer group were involved with him in these infractions. Pete's adjustment in school was very poor. His probation officer felt his offenses were the result "of a personal problem of the boy and his lack of understanding of himself." Pete appeared to resent his father and also had difficulty in adjusting to the type of community in which he was living.

GEORGE: George was involved in sniffing airplane glue on many occasions. He had also been apprehended for consumption of alcoholic beverages and was suspected in various automobile larcenies. He was seventeen years old at the time of his admission.

This boy had excessive group loyalties which were often detrimental to his own position and welfare, and he would not reveal any information to the police nor make any admissions. His parents had no understanding of his misbehavior and antisocial activities.

LEE: The youngest boy in the group was a husky, blond youth named Lee, who was nearly eighteen at the time of admission. His father was deceased and his mother was a medical secretary who was born in Germany.

For several years prior to his admission, Lee was involved in various breaking and entry charges and one runaway episode. His school work was barely passing and his most important interest was his fifteen-year-old girlfriend.

Lee was diagnosed as a constricted boy who felt little anxiety and bottled up his sense of inadequacy. He always managed to divorce himself from any real involvement with others. However, he was felt to be a boy capable of amiability, thoughtfulness, cooperativeness, and politeness, and his prognosis was generally favorable.

During the early stages, the group had no group structure. Instead, it was an aggregate of individuals basically divided into two factions. The four oldest boys, three of whom had arrived within a two-day period, constituted the first faction. The leader of this clique was a tough, aggressive, somewhat bullyish narcotics user named Rich, who for reasons to be described shortly was not considered a part of this group. His compatriots were Harry, Bill and Eddie.

The second faction was led by Pete. The other members of that clique were George and Lee. These three boys had been admitted together from the same county and thus knew each other prior to their arrival.

Mike and Craig could be considered isolates in that they chose to remain aloof from all the other members of the group, whereas Art served as the scapegoat for the group, and was excluded from membership in both of the two factions.

The early sessions of Group Six consisted of hostile, defensive behavior, primarily on the part of Rich. Lip service to conventional standards came from Harry and to some extent from Eddie. The early sessions were primarily taken up by the telling of stories and the assignment of problems by the group. Telling stories means that each boy had to describe in detail to the group all the delinquent activities in which he had been involved, whether or not he had been caught for them. He also had to describe and discuss his relationships with his family, what he had done in school, etc.

Early in July, Rich and Eddie brought narcotics into the facility, in the form of glue and barbiturates. Following a typical delinquent pattern, they refused to admit this either to the staff or to their group. Because of this they were returned to juvenile court. This was done to impress upon them the seriousness of their behavior and also to make an impact upon their group. They and their peers had to learn that in order for them to benefit from the program, it was absolutely necessary that they discuss their delinquency in the group sessions. This they could do and remain immune from punishment. This immunity must be maintained if the necessary trust relationship within the group is to be developed. The group must serve a rehabilitative and not a punitive purpose. After a period of time, Rich and Eddie were returned to the program.

The group did not begin to develop a complete structure until the latter part of August when the oldest boys were already at the facility two months. It was also at this time that Rich was again returned to court as unsuitable for the program. This decision was made because Rich was obstructing the formation of a group structure and was interfering with the attempts of the other boys to help themselves and each other. He had not gained from his previous experience and had decided that he liked what he was and was not going to attempt to change. Occasionally a case arises in which a boy appears to be a suitable candidate for the program on the surface but simply proves not to be amenable to this particular approach. In that case it is better to remove the individual than it is to allow him to destroy the necessary group culture.

As the group passed through the stage of revealing themselves and their feelings about each other, the members began to identify with their group and to recognize the fact that demands were being made upon them to help make group decisions. This was also the time during which the basic decision was made to change or not to change. Art was still divorced from the group, partly because of his low status and partly through his own choices.

As Group Six entered its third stage, Rich was gone. Harry and Bill came more and more to assume the leadership of their group, partly because they were the two oldest boys. The lines were much less clearly drawn between the two cliques, and George was emerging as one of the most influential members of the group. The fundamental basis of influence in the meeting was changing from deviant to non-deviant, and Bill and George were making the greatest progress in that direction. Mike and Craig became much more involved in their group.

Late in September, Harry asked the group to discuss how he had solved his problems and his readiness to go home. Harry believed that all his problems stemmed from his being easily "mislead," and because he had solved this he had solved his other problems as well. However, his reasons were weak and were not based, for the most part, upon what he had been doing at Ocean, therefore, they were rejected by the group. When the group did finally vote on Harry's request, he received a "yes" vote from all but Craig who felt he didn't know enough about him. Craig's vote perhaps best told the story of Harry and his progress toward solving his problems. Harry never really did go beyond the plateau he had reached, but he was discharged in October. Bill was also discharged at the same time, but in his case a great deal of progress had occurred. An extract from his final monthly report indicates the following: "Bill had a good final month in residence at Ocean. His dependency and immaturity, very evident upon his arrival all but disappeared during the latter part of his residence. He now seems very capable of dealing with all his problems and difficulties."

All the members of the group participated actively during this stage. They became genuine members of the group, and as this occurred, they were being alienated from previous delinquent group affiliations. Art was perhaps the only group member who didn't fall into this pattern. He was unpopular with and not accepted by his peers. He had no status and was consigned to remain a scapegoat. The group leader constantly had to interject himself in order to protect Art from being overwhelmed, and also to prevent the group from spending all its time discussing him and his problems.

An example of the group members' attempts to absolve themselves of previous delinquent associations was the case of Mike. Mike expressed the wish to have his buddies think he was the same old Mike. He wanted to change and yet he wanted to remain the same. Mike was being pressured by the group to make a choice between his old friends and new friends, i.e. between delinquency and non-delinquency.

In the final stage, Group Six directly attacked and resolved the problems of its members. Art was attacked for his lying. Pete on his use of narcotics, aggravation and "tough guy" problems, etc. During this period the leader performed only a minimal role, his major function being to sharpen the assault on the problems of group members and to emphasize the alternatives to delinquent behavior.

Role reversal was also evident during this last period, specifically between Art and Craig. These boys were unable to form a friendly relationship, but instead were constantly arguing, bickering, and becoming annoyed with each other. In order to alleviate this situation somewhat, the leader encouraged them to reverse roles, assume the identity of the other person, and attempt to see situations through the other person's eyes. This was accomplished with favorable results.

As the group accomplished its objectives, it began to send its members home. Eddie and Craig left in November, and the remainder of the group in December. Art was the last to be discharged. Following are parts of the final reports on these boys. It should be noted that these reports are prepared for the boys and the group, and are presented orally to them. Certain points in the reports are included and phrased in a particular way for therapeutic impact.

HARRY: "Harry had an above average final month in residence at Ocean . . . Harry's participation in the group sessions did not increase during his last month. He seemed to be content to mark time in order to find out what was going to happen to him . . . He became more involved with and more interested in helping his peers than at any other time during his stay."

BILL: "Bill had a good final month in residence at Ocean. His dependence and immaturity, very evident upon his arrival, all but disappeared during the latter part of his residence . . . Bill is an active participant in the group sessions, and has played a big part in helping the other boys cope with their problems. He supports them when he feels they are right, but will attack them when he feels they are wrong. Bill's interest in doing this seems very sincere."

EDDIE: "Eddie's final month in residence was a vast improvement over his first three months . . . if he is sincere in his beliefs and attitudes, and his reasons are enough to keep him out of trouble on the outside, this is all that really matters. Only time will tell whether or not this is the case."

MIKE: "Mike had an above average fourth month in residence at Ocean . . . participation in the group sessions is erratic, which perhaps reflects his attitudes. His relationship with adults is good, and he is considered to be a good worker by his supervisors."

CRAIG: "Contrary to what he had shown previously, Craig indicated that he did know what was happening and that he had sound ideas and alternates for dealing with his problems and the problems of his peers . . . Craig became an active participant and even somewhat of a leader in the group sessions. His contributions were, for the most part, very worthwhile."

ART: "Art had an average final month in residence. In terms of what other boys were able to accomplish, Art's behavior and attitudes still left much to be desired. On the face of it, however, this boy appeared to progress as far as his capabilities would allow."

PETE: "Pete had an average final month in residence at Ocean. He doesn't seem to have made any great changes in his behavior and attitudes over his last reporting period . . . Pete participates actively in the group sessions and again is able to assume very well the role of a 'helped' boy. He becomes aggravated, vengeful, and then withdrawn when the group refuses to accept his ideas."

GEORGE: "George's active participation in the group sessions was directed sharply to the delinquent behavior and attitudes of the other boys. This was true to such an extent that George would become aggravated when his ideas and solutions were not readily accepted. It is in such situations that George's tendency to be a tough guy comes to the surface."

LEE: "Lee had a good final month in residence. His awareness of his own problems and of the problems of other boys reached its highest point, and perhaps more important, his awareness of how to handle these problems became clearly evident. Lee was much involved with the other boys during his last month, and his change in attitude and behavior was clearly discernible."

Assessment of Group Six

In the brief, simplified look at the history of Group Six at Ocean, it is possible to see that the group did follow the different stages of development. Also, one can get an idea of how the group delineates, attacks, and finally solves the problems of its members.

During the group sessions, the leader attempts to support and assist the group in becoming aware of its problems, as well as to make interpretations of the interaction between members. Group members will openly and defiantly test the leader's definition of the guided group interaction situation and his role in it. The hostile and aggressive reactions of the boys require a special type of leadership and ability. The leader usually handles aggressive reactions by turning them back to the group for their discussion. The leader's attitude must be one of acceptance, and he must not inflict punitive or counter-aggressive acts which would lead to condemnation of the boys themselves. He simply asks provocative questions, repeats ideas expressed in the group, and summarizes to bring out significant issues.

Turning to the role of the participants in guided group interaction, each person must, according to his ability, make some contribution to the maintenance of the group. They must be able to deal with each other, and work or exchange opinions with each other without hurting each other too much. This is very difficult to accomplish when the group has a scapegoat similar to Art who becomes a target.

Each person must evolve his own role in the group, understand his present role, and attempt to develop new roles. He must make the crucial choice that in order to survive in the community he must change his values, attitudes and behavior. Each member of the group learns that he helps himself by helping other group members.

Guided group interaction requires an easy, informal environment where members are democratic equals and where social controls evolve out of interaction and increased understandings. There are no formal rules or punishments imposed by the group leader, and the effort to establish such rules with accompanying punishments by the group itself should be discouraged. If allowed to develop, these can become the focus of the group's efforts rather than real behavior change. Rules and punishments can also become a method through which stronger group members subjugate weaker ones.

The sessions alone do not operate in a vacuum. There is a social world outside the meeting that is equally important in achieving the goals of the program. It is this outside social world that provides support for the meetings. The experiences provide the raw data for discussions of group and personal problems. Since the theoretical orientation of the program is focused on the "here and now" experiences of the boys and the people with whom they interact, every other kind of experience plays a part in the rehabilitation of the population. The informal norms and sanctions that govern social relationships should change with each group as it goes through the program.

As each boy leaves the residential group center, he is asked to record his impressions of his career, both in the community and in the program. Not all boys are able or willing to do so. However, most of the boys comply and prepare a statement of their impressions. The following stories were recorded by the boys in Group Six upon their release to the community. It is felt these will serve very effectively as a self-measure of the impact of the program upon the boys.

HARRY: "My first impression of Ocean when I arrived was the same as everyone else's I presume. That is, being I had no thought of helping myself before I came here, I couldn't understand the boys that were here when I arrived. I couldn't see how they could look as if they were trying to help themselves when on the outside you never even dream of how seriously wrong you have been going about life. About what sorrows and regrets you are putting yourself through. But what's more is how the people you love and those who love and respect you are being affected by your wrong mistakes. And the people you do the wrong to are being very much affected by what you did to them. I am positive now though, that by being sent here is the best way of straightening out juveniles. Up here in Ocean you have the understanding and help of other boys and mainly the advantage of time to reason and think solely of the reasoning these other boys give you. I feel that on the outside there is no serious thinking and the time to really think because there is where all the temptations are and the way you are going about things will continue because of the temptations and unreasonable time. But as I have just said in a previous statement in this paragraph I positive that here in Ocean is the best thing that can happen to a juvenile in the fact that here you have understanding help and reasonable time the reasons for leading a clean life."

BILL: "When I first came up to Ocean I looked around and knew this place wasn't for me. When I meet some of the kids I was almost sure that they were bullshiting. I didn't think that anybody could help themself. But I found out later that you could. So I tried to help myself and I did but I was sure went I first came up here that it couldn't be done. I am glad that I didn't go back to court. Now I think that this place is the best place for any boy that has gotten in trouble. When I leave this place I know that I will make good on the outside."

EDDIE: "When I first came to Ocean I thought the place was big joke. I thought that all the guys were good-goodys and fags; and that they were all playing the role. I figures that this place couldn't help me or anybody else. The check system got me agrivated because I couldn't see any sense in it.

"Now I feel that this place can help anyone who wants it to, it helped me. The check system, not only is good for making a person realize what he is doing but also for finding out what he is real like. The meetings are the main factor in helping people, because when a delinquent is told by another delinquent what he is doing wrong it means more than an adult. The one thing I disagree with is that this place is suppose to be run by the boys; but there is not one inclination of this. I think if the boys were given more of a chance to run the place, even in little ways, the boys might be able to be helped earlier. I feel that boys who come up here for drugs might be easily discouraged because the boys & the supervisors try to make them feel that drugs can not be helped. I feel that if the boys down here for drugs were given half a chance & not brainwashed into thinking they cannot be helped, more junkes could be helped. Another thing I disagree with is that Annandale is held over the boys head to much & this might force boys into playing the role. If other points were stressed more than Annandale less people would play the role which would lead into more people being helped. Something that gets me agrivated is the shit that a person in one meeting can't help a person in another meeting because he is said not to be interested in his own meetings. We are put up here to help us people, so why are we given hell for try to help each other? This deceiving us, & sometimes a person from a different meeting can be more of a help because of the simulating of their problems and background."

MIKE: "When I first got here I thought the groups were a bunch of punks and good-goodies and this place wasnit the place for me but after a few days I found out different. I thought the check system was all fucked up. But after someone explained it I thought I would like to be helped so I went to work on it. Before I cam up I wanted to stay out of trouble but I went about it the wrong way on the outside. But being up here made me find out the right way to do this. I was told that the boys ran this place but later found out different. I thought that if you were voted out you would go home or on furlought but I guess not but that wasn't all that bad. I didn't mind the work at all because I liked most of it. I liked all the staff members except for Lead Ball. (A college student who spent the summer working as a seasonal assistant.) But that was my fault because I made a wise remark to him one day after that he disliked me. That taight me not to wise off. Also I disliked to do house cleaning. I also didn't think this place could help anybody that was what everybody said but I found out different.

I changed my ways of thinking altogether now. I think just about any body can be helped if they really want to help themselves. After being here a week or so I learned how to go about helping myself and how it changed me. I was talking to my probation officer and he noticed a change in me. I was only about 1 month old so that made me feel good. My parents saw a change also. I think this place is run about the best way it could be run and I don't think if a person can't be helped, there is no other place that can help him. I think Mr. Rose should be more strick on the boys because they are taking advantage of him to much. (Jay Rose was the Work Supervisor at the Ocean Residential Group Center.) By asking for cigarette breaks and so on. Otherwise I think everything is run alrite. I don't think it is his fault because he is trying to be a nice guy but instead he is getting fucked around. I think the whole prograne set me up for my future because I have a lot more risonsibility now. In many way work, and being a good respictible person. I think I can do that now. So I think that this place is the only type of institution that is of any help to a delinquent and that places like Jamesburg and Annandale are no good to reform a person. I think they only make you worse than wat you were when you first got into trouble. I think that the meetings do the most for a boy because if you think something is minor like I did the meeting can change that because it did for me. I think the meeting can change almost anything that has to do with delinquency even late shit."

CRAIG: "*The first Cuple Weeks Here.* Well the day I arrived here, I though this place was a little cookie, I mean to me everybody was playing the roll. Everytime I did something rong someone was always checking me, at the time I didn't really know it was for my own good, I though they were trying to get me into trouble. When they would talk to me I would get wise, and try to start a fight with them. I though in my own mind people were trying to mess me up. The reason why I though this place was faged out when I came here is because the guys were checking me for everything I did rong. and because I couldn't clown around. I always used to clown and I wasen't used to stoping. Well I can't think of any more to say for the first cuple weeks.

The Rest of my time Here. Well after I found out people were trying to help me. it made me think a lot about this place. I never paid attenchen in the meeting for a long I never said anything because I was afride I would get someone in trouble. But when I was a month an a half people were trying to help me. the talk problems with me. So I decided to try in help my self. I think matter in fack I got all my problems solved except for the following.

Clown. The reason why I didn't get my clown problem solved, is sertain times I feel I half to clown around with someone. to keep me out of bad moods and maybe get some one else out of bad moods.

Wise. Sure I get wise but when I get wise I think in my own mind it is helping me from getting aggervated at anyone. Other times I do it to clown. thata shy I know I didn't solve my wise guy problems, but as far as my other problems are concerned I did solve them. and I want to thank my meeting for helping me do it. and I am going to do my best to shown then I am helped. I want to thank mister Finckenhawer and mister Reagon for everything they did for me. (Vincent J. Regan was the Superintendent of the Ocean Residential Group Center at this time.) they are the two nicest guy you ever want to meet. Well that all I half to say."

ART: "When I first came here I thought that this place was pretty nice because to me it was a hundred percent better than county jail. But after awhile I started hating the place because everygody found out what I really am and that meant that they knew I was a liar and they were getting on my back quite a lot about it and I was getting quite aggrivated because I didn't want to tell anybody I was lying because I was ashamed about it and I didn't want to confess about it because I thought everybody would look down on me. But the thing that really made me start liking the place is that I started realizing that everybody was really trying to help me and when they had proof I was lying they tried to help me instead of teasing the hell out of me. I feel that the system this place has is very good because the people here make me think a lot and go by my own decisions. I feel that if it wasn't for this place I wouldn't have had enough courage to make my own decisions because I would be scared to mess myself up, loke on a job. For a while I thought to myself that Mr. Regan was just playing a hard tough roll, but now I realize that if I couldn't have taken it from Mr. Regan I couldn't have taken it from a boss on a job. Actually though, even though I don't express myself to well, I'm very grateful to Mr. Regan for what he did to me because he taight me the true meaning of responsibility by giving me punishment when I couldn't except responsibility. He and all the other members of the staff taught me to think for myself and to think before I do something. I feel that my main reason of why I got into trouble is because I never thought about the consiquences and I never thought about other people because I just wanted to be a big shot and show off in front of everybody. However, I found out from this place that I can get along just as well with people just by being my normal self. I feel that in a way I owe my future to all the people here because thier the ones that really made me change my mind to change my ways and begin a new beginning. I only hope that a lot of other kids get the break I got."

PETE: "When I first arrived at Ocean I thought I knew pretty much about the place. I was wrong. My opinion about the older boys was that they were playing the role and I couldn't be changed.

My opinion of the place really changed when I was about two months old on my second furlough. I drank and after I drank I was mad at myself from then on my reasons had a lot more meaning. I did at times act good just for the sake of looking good, but, I'm leaving with greater confidence in myself with an honest pity on my friends and my brother who get in trouble. I used to think they were great but now I feel sorry for them.'

GEORGE: "When I first came up here I wanted to be helped but the way they went about it didn't go over to well. With its check system and the work I never had a job on the outside cause I was to lazy to go out and work now I think I can do better on the outside cause of this experience.

When I first came here I didn't get along with everyone to well I had a big mouth I got agravated real easy and I didn't like people to say stuff like critizing me this was the hardest thing to solve I didnt solve it all the way but I realized what I was doing and I soped. Then some of the guy I didnt get along with I started getting along with better I think this is a pretty important thing in life, getting along with people.

This place started me doing something I never did be for giveng in and exepting critizism with out getting pissed off at people.

I didnt have a flunky problem but Mr. Regan pointed out something that stoped me from some future bust. he remarked on how I used to get mixed up in my friends quarrels.

Some thing else mr finkenhuaer said in arty about there are problemes are all naginfied in arty then I though about it and it made sence so I tried to change those things.

When I get on the outside Im going to hang around with my friend who dont get busted cause that way I can never get pushed or triped into any thing.

Another thining I could neve make the right dision so I was scard to make them now at least I try to think for my self.

I think my worst problems were my family and sniffing I going to get along better with my family now and I no Ill never sniff again I realize how stupid it was. my parent are alway worring about me no I going to worry about them."

LEE: "Most guys, when they first get here, think that they got a rotten deal by being sent here. I guess that's the way that I felt too but I realize now that these past four months have been the most important months of my life. I admit that Ive been slick, but I guess everyone has (and I'm not using that as an excuse thought I'm only saying what's on my mind). I've benefitted, and I think that most guys benefit from this program in one way or another. Unfortunately some guys benefit in the wrong way because some guys just don't want to go strat and nothing will ever change their minds. I think that if everyone was sent to this place there wouldn't be need for as many reformatories and jails as their are. I guess I don't have anything else to say, just that this place helped me and will always stay with me."

Epilogue of Group Six

Each boy released from the residential group centers is returned to probation status in the community, and a post release adjustment report is completed by his probation officer between six months and eighteen months following his release. Six months is considered to be the crucial time period for readjustment in the community.

The post release adjustment reports on the same boys in Group Six reflected the following:

HARRY: Harry did not appear in court for a new violation or offense following his release, and was discharged from probation supervision with improvement. His overall adjustment was considered good and he was working full time. The probation officer felt that the experience of residence in the group center had been of definite value to Harry.

BILL: Bill was discharged from probation without improvement, and his overall adjustment was considered to be poor although he had apparently committed no new violations or offenses. The probation officer felt that Bill's experience at the group center was of some value to him.

EDDIE: Eddie was committed to the New Jersey Reformatory for Males at Annandale about three months after discharge. He was charged with possession of narcotic paraphernalia and consorting with a narcotic user. Seven months later Eddie was recalled from Annandale by the juvenile court judge and continued on probation. At that time he enrolled as a 12th grade student in the local high school.

MIKE: Mike was still under probation supervision at the time of the report. He had appeared in court again for drunkenness on six occasions, and was being treated at the New Jersey Neuro-Psychiatric Clinic. Despite these problems, his overall adjustment following release from the group center was considered good, and the probation officer felt that his experience had been of definite value to Mike.

CRAIG: Craig was still under probation supervision at the time of the report. He had appeared in juvenile court again for possession of alcohol, and his probation was continued. His overall adjustment was considered good; he was working part time;

and he was actively seeking additional employment. The probation officer felt that the experience of residence in the group
center had been of definite value to Craig.

ART: Art was committed to the Annandale Reformatory for auto
theft three weeks after his release from Ocean. He had returned
to Ocean on a Sunday evening approximately two weeks after
his discharge for a visit. At that time he was driving a second
hand car which he indicated had been bought for him by his
father. Although he emphasized how well he was doing, he
seemed nervous and apprehensive, particularly when he volun-
tarily explained in detail about the car. It was discovered later
that the car in fact had been stolen, and Art was committed
for this theft on the following Friday. It seems, in retrospect,
almost as if he were reaching out for help and wanted to be
challenged and helped in his wrongdoing just as he had in the
guided group sessions.

After serving a period of time at Annandale, Art, while on
a preparole release status during his final month was assigned
the task of painting the home of the assistant superintendent,
along with several other boys. The other boys apparently
talked Art into running away. He was caught and subsequently
committed to the Bordentown Reformatory for Males (an institution for older, more sophisticated offenders).

Representing one of the two most evident failures from
this group, Art's inability to resist being mislead and to adhere
to socially acceptable behavior would point toward evidence
of psychopathic tendencies. Because of this, the guided group
sessions did not impact upon him except on a superficial level.
He was able to verbalize the characteristics of a "helped" boy
as evidenced by his self-description, but he was not able to behave accordingly. Art represents a good example of the need
in the groups to get below this superficial level and to divert
into another type of treatment effort those who cannot profit
from guided group interaction.

PETE: Pete was still under probation supervision and had appeared in juvenile court again for possession of beer. His pro-

bation had been continued at that time. Pete's overall adjustment was considered to be good and he was attending school at the time of the report. The officer felt that Pete's experience had been of definite value to him.

GEORGE: George was under probation supervision at the time of the report. He had been charged with assault and was scheduled to appear in New York Criminal Court. Although he had reenrolled in school, he again dropped out and was currently working full time. The probation officer felt he had made an average overall adjustment, and that the group center had been of some value to George.

LEE: Lee had violated probation for an unstipulated offense and was continued on probation. His overall adjustment following release from the group center was considered very good. He was attending school and working part time. The probation officer felt that the experience of residence in the group center had been of definite value to Lee.

With the exception of the two obvious failures, Eddie and Art, and despite some other more or less marginal adjustments, the consensus of opinions of the probation officers who supervised these boys before and after their group center experience was that it had been of value to them. This is a good example of the intangibles involved in changing human behavior. Significant changes in attitudes and outlook might occur even with occasional early relapses in behavior patterns. The post-release adjustment of the group is also a good example, and this is offered only partially as an excuse, of the results of inexperience and resort to trial and error learning on the part of the group leader.

The implications of the Highfields concept for the rehabilitation of young offenders cannot be over-emphasized. It may also be a progressive form of prevention for coping with predelinquents as well. New programs, utilizing guided group interaction, could be designed for this purpose and might open new avenues for the prevention and control of juvenile delinquency.

The operating model described has been successfully modified from time to time, so that each program develops features designed to meet its particular set of problems. However, the concept that the peer group can be used in effecting change in the attitudes and behavior patterns of adolescents must remain intact. Adolescents have the potential for change and for dealing with their own problems as well as the problems of others. The group approach using guided group interaction is one effective method for developing this potential.

BIBLIOGRAPHY

Elias, Albert: The Highfields program for juvenile delinquents. Unpublished report, March, 1961.

Elias, Albert: A reply to some unanswered questions about Highfields. *Am Correction, 21:* no. 4, 1959.

McCorkle, Lloyd W., Elias, Albert, Bixby, F. Lovell: *The Highfields Story.* New York, Henry Holt and Co., 1958.

McCorkle, Lloyd W.: Group therapy in the treatment of offenders, *Fed Probation, 16:*22–27, 1952.

Sherwood, Clarence C., and Walker, William S. Some unanswered questions about Highfields. Ann Arbor, Univ Mich Pr, 1959.

Chapter 11

SPECIFIC OBJECTIVES FOR THE INSTITUTIONAL TREATMENT OF JUVENILES

Dean Edwards [*]

- ■ Why We Have Institutions
- ■ Programs, But No Program
- ■ The Team Approach
- ■ What, How, and Who
- ■ A Model for Implementation
- ■ Conclusions
- ■ Bibliography

"I F you don't know where you are going, how do you know when you get there?" is an apt question that can directly apply to the programming that exists in many institutions that supposedly function for the purpose of "rehabilitating" the juvenile offender. Specific, practical, goal-directed programming is often absent. Instead, there may exist a statement of philosophy that is quite vague and abounding in generalities, and which cannot serve as a directional and guiding force in the rehabilitative process.

* Edwards, Dean, Specific objectives for the institutional treatment of juveniles, *Federal Probation*, September 1971, Vol. 35, #3, p. 26–29. Reprinted with permission.

Why We Have Institutions

Basically, an institution for juvenile offenders exists for two purposes. One of these is the temporary custody of the individual in order to protect society from his transgressions. Sometimes this aspect is overemphasized, and sometimes it is underemphasized.

While recognizing the importance of the custody aspect, it has been stated that, "this does not mean we must become so custody concerned that we fail to utilize to the full the other features of our treatment program. As has already been pointed out, custody alone does not protect the public except for the relatively short time while the individual is confined.

Dr. Arnold Richards (1968) emphasizes the need for developing programs in institutions which aim to produce change in the chronic offender. He writes: "As long as we cannot keep the recidivist locked up for his whole life we can only fulfill our obligation to the security of society by changing the individual."

The second purpose of the institution, then, is to "restore the confined offender to the mainstream of society." This is generally covered by the term "rehabilitation." This term tends to have moral connotations. Perhaps a better term is "reintegration," which simply means getting the juvenile restored to society where he can live within an acceptable framework of the existing civil and criminal laws, even if he is not "one hundred percent moral."

This point is made because it is now apparent that a youth might function quite well in a given subculture, but be at odds with general middle-class values. The statement is made that "a prevailing emphasis on delinquency as a problem of personality defect, psychic or otherwise, has led society to neglect important structural conditions, both social and cultural, which are relevant to an understanding of such behavior. Especially neglected have been efforts to take such conditions into account in the study of individual cases." (Martin 1968)

The fact that institutions in general have not been overly successful in their function of restoring the offender to society can be seen by the high rate of recidivism that prevails. The question is, then, can anything be done to improve the job that institutions are doing?

One "out" for the institutional people is to deny that the fault is theirs, and to project the blame on the field, or parole staff. The first sentence in a booklet published by the Children's Bureau states that "Juvenile correctional experts agree that the successful rehabilitation of institutionalized delinquent youth depends *primarily* [emphasis mine] upon the availability of quality post-institutional services." (Manella 1967) The implication here—though perhaps not intended—is either that the role of the institution is relatively unimportant or that institutions are doing their job adequately, and that when the juvenile is released, changes have been made that make him ready to live in society, provided the aftercare services are adequate.

Probably neither of these is correct. The role of the institution *is* important—as is the role of postinstitutional services, but it is also quite probable that the institutions are not doing their job adequately.

Programs, But No Program

It is a seeming paradox that many institutions have fine programs, *but no program*. There may be a modern school building with excellent facilities, a good social service staff with great organization, a cottage-life department with regular inservice training, *but no overall, coordinating set of objectives that comprise a program*.

The need is not unrecognized. Leighton W. Dudley (1966) spells it out when he states that:

> A program is needed that will insure on his (youthful offender) departure he has the capacity to relate significantly to family and friends, that he has the basic academic and vocational skills he needs, and that he will have sufficient confidence in himself to translate a successful institutional experience into a successful community experience.

If such a program existed, the next step would be to get the various disciplines within the institution to coordinate their activities. Basically, the different disciplines within an institution should operate like a human hand. They often do this now, but with the flow being *outward* from the wrist, with each digit representing a discipline, such as education, social services, cottage life, etc., and *with each doing its own thing.* There may be surface elements of cooperation, and good will, but no real unifying force because there are no unifying, clear-cut institutional objectives.

The Team Approach

The directional flow must be reversed, with each digit still representing a discipline, but with the input being toward the wrist, and the wrist representing unifying objectives which have been devised to produce the desired finished product. Hopefully, this will be expedited by the effect of "multiple-impact."

Such a "team-approach" to the treatment of juvenile offenders is not new, but its widespread implementation has not been forthcoming. As might be expected, it is more likely to be found in smaller institutions than in larger ones.

Carle F. O'Neal (1965) writing in *Federal Probation,* urges that the separate teams must fuse. Regarding the separation of custody and treatment, he states that "custody (care and control) is a basic part of treatment, and the basic principles of treatment (relationship, honesty, and limit-setting) are essential to enlightened custody."

There has been a great deal written about this need for the various services to coordinate their activities. Dudley (1960), while recognizing the advances made in facilities and the high quality of personnel staffing them, nevertheless points out that:

> We have not learned enough yet as to how we are to fit all these people together into one cohesive dynamic team—a team that can recognize the wide variety of problems and needs among youthful offenders, and provide the kind of experience and treatment that a particular offender must have before he is ready to return to the community with real hope for a successful adjustment.

Gerald Wittman (1965) recognizes the importance of involving the total hierarchy on the team when he writes that:

There is a tendency on the part of some persons to regard the psychiatrist, the social worker, and the psychologist as the institutional treatment team. While these professionals are essential, treatment extends beyond the infrequent interviews scheduled between the clientele of the training school and those staff members with graduate degrees in one or another of the helping professions. In order to be effective, treatment goals need to be all pervasive. All staff, regardless of responsibilities, need to be a part of the rehabilitation process.

Dr. Richard Jessor (1965) discussing the Englewood Project in *Re-Educating Confined Delinquents*, takes a similar unifying approach. He explains that the trend has been to think of the total institutional experience as educational in nature; and to attribute educational functions to all personnel who deal with inmates, whether as quarters officers, work supervisors, recreational leaders, or whatever.

Thus it can be seen that there is a lot of dialogue concerning the importance of the team approach and the merging of the disciplines. But the disciplines cannot merge unless there is a force that is conducive to merger. Talk won't do it. And the magnetic field of a vague statement of institutional philosophy is too weak. Something much more concrete is needed. That something is the development of specific objectives and the definition of goals.

This critical aspect is cogently summed up by Street, Vinter, and Perrow (1966) who write that "definition and specification of the mission or essential productive task of the institution are primary tasks of the executive, *necessary to give purpose and direction to staff activity and to earn support from external units.*" (Emphasis, mine)

What, How, and Who

Basically, the entire problem of assisting delinquent youth can be oversimplified to revolve around two simple questions. These are:

1. What do we want to accomplish with these youth?
2. How do we do it?

These questions must be answered in their numerical order.

There is no point in discussing program—how to do it—if we do not know *specifically* what it is that we want to accomplish.

Phase I, then, is the development of objectives that are geared toward the minimum goal of changing the behavior of the delinquent youth to the extent that he will be able to function in society. (Often it is mistakenly assumed that this has happened because he had demonstrated an ability to function *within the institution.*) Each objective should be: (1) specific in nature, and lend itself to the development of a program for its attainment and (2) such that its attainment will contribute toward the goal of enabling the individual to function adequately *outside* the institution.

It is the writer's contention that the "Developmental Tasks for Delinquents," listed below, will meet these criteria.

DEVELOPMENTAL TASKS FOR DELINQUENTS

1. To become familiar with the process whereby rules, regulations, and laws have evolved, and *why.*
2. To initiate planning which will enable one to live within the framework of society's civil and criminal laws, and thus earn the rights and privileges which accompany living in a free society.
3. To attain a maximum degree of self-understanding, recognizing one's own strengths and weaknesses.
4. To initiate planning for occupational selection.
5. To set realistic educational goals and to begin planning and implementing accordingly.
6. To plan for the acquisition of material things in a realistic societal-condoned manner.
7. To understand the physiological, sociological, and psychological aspects of male-female relationships, and to determine a set of appropriate values.
8. To control impulsive behavior, and to give rational consideration before acting.
9. To be accepting of others, and to recognize their right to live their particular way of life, as long as it is within the framework of law, order, and justice.
10. To expand one's thinking beyond the self, and to give

consideration to providing, to some degree, service to one's fellow man.

After objectives, or goals, or "developmental tasks" have been formulated, the admittedly much more difficult task is to implement them by developing a program which will lead to the assimilation of those objectives by the delinquent youth. This is Phase II —"how do we do it?"

Concurrent with the development of the program must be a delineation and coordination of responsibility among the disciplines. Some tasks might be the prime responsibility of the school setting, the cottage or the social services section. Others might evolve from individual and group settings with a psychologist. However, although a particular objective might be the prime responsibility of a specific department, all other departments would be aware of the total program, and reinforce each other at every opportunity.

A Model for Implementation

Combining with this team approach to create a "multiple-impact" can be a combination of mental approaches, using intellectual, rational, and emotional aspects. One example of how the multiple-impact, multiple-approach combination might be utilized with a "developmental task" is given below:

No. 1.—TO BECOME FAMILIAR WITH THE PROCESS WHEREBY RULES, REGULATIONS, AND LAWS HAVE EVOLVED, AND WHY.

A. School-intellectual approach.
Use of available filmstrips, reference material, and text-book material depicting how man has banded together with others.
How the need for rules evolved, and the benefits.
B. Cottage-rational approach.
a. Discussions of the need for rules in group living. Why specific rules are needed.
b. Examples of disordered situations that would exist in cottages without rules. (It might be feasible to develop

own teaching aids, staging a disordered cottage situation and filming with 8 mm. or preparing video tapes.)

C. Recreation-rational approach.

   a. Examples of needs for rules in sports. Use of a specific sport. For example, demonstrate rules of basketball. Show how violations of rules eliminate individual skills.

   b. Discuss how even professional athletes—football players, boxers—must adhere to rules.

D. School-rational approach.

Law enforcement. Use available commercial film-strip, *The Teenager and the Police: Conflict and Paradox.* Show film showing routine job of a policeman. Have a police officer meet with class for a discussion.

E. Cottage and Social Worker-emotional approach.

Using emotional impact, show possible consequences of rules violations. Use a highway patrol film showing actual scenes of death, mutilation, serious injury, including sounds, as a result of violating traffic laws. Project the victims as being the parents, friends, or relatives of the juvenile.

Implementing such a program within an existing institution would be no easy thing. A tremendous amount of cooperation would be required among the various disciplines—cooperation that is not always easy to come by. The educational system would have to accept the fact that it is not the "sun" of the institutional "solar system," and the personnel in the social services department would have to keep their heads out of the clouds and their feet on the ground. Cottage life people would have to accept a role beyond that of custodial supervision of wards.

Means of grouping the juveniles would have to be devised for certain aspects of the program. Based on size of the institution and intake conditions, this might have to be intercottage in nature. A means of student accounting would have to be devised to insure exposure to all aspects of the program. And in regard to success or failure, a systematic followup procedure would be necessary to determine the usefulness of the program and to make modifications if indicated.

Conclusions

Does the implementation of such a program imply a solution to juvenile corrections? Probably not, although possibly so, at least to some extent. On the one hand, human behavior is quite complicated, and it is not expected that "reformed" individuals can be turned out as in a factory. The cause of delinquency is not always known, and thus we do not have a standard raw material.

On the other hand, perhaps we spend too much time looking for the cause and not enough time looking for the cure. By analogy, if a person is admitted to the emergency room with a severe gash on his arm, the physician does not immediately concern himself with whether the wound was caused by a switchblade knife or a piece of falling sheet metal, or whether it was caused by design or accident. The wound is there, and he follows a procedure in treating it.

It is just possible that a similar system would work in juvenile corrections—that long-range behavioral changes might be accomplished, and the adolescent might be reached by specific programming—not all delinquents, but a much larger percentage than is presently reached by willy-nilly programming.

The task would be difficult, but a motivating factor would be the realization on the part of the staff—*all* staff—that they *do* have a function in the process of reintegration.

In summary, vague statements of philosophy are useless. Needed are the development and implementation of specific objectives that will provide direction to, and use the potential of, all staff members. It's time to get objective about objectives.

BIBLIOGRAPHY

Dudley, Leighton W.: New horizons for the institutional treatment of youth offenders. *Fed Probation*, 30:50, 1966.
Institutional Treatment of Younger Offenders: El Reno, Oklahoma: Federal Reformatory, p. 13, 1965.
Jessor, Richard: *Re-Educating Confined Delinquents.* Washington, D. C.: U. S. Department of Justice, p. 3, 1965.

Manella, Raymond L.: *Post-Institutional Services for Delinquent Youth.* Washington, D. C.: U. S. Department of Health, Education and Welfare, p. 1, 1967.

Martin, John M., Fitzpatrick, Joseph P., and Gould, Robert: *Analyzing Delinquent Behavior—A New Approach.* Washington, D. C.: U. S. Department of Health, Education and Welfare, p. 5, 1968.

O'Neal, Carle F.: Professional and custodial staff must merge their treatment efforts. *Fed Probation*, 29:45, 1965.

Richards, Arnold: Clinicians views on correctional education. *Supplement to Re-Educating Confined Delinquents.* Washington, D. C.: Federal Bureau of Prisons, p. 28, 1968.

Street, David, Vinter, Robert D., and Pervow, Charles: *Organization for Treatment.* New York, The Free Press, p. 48, 1966.

Wittman, Gerald P.: Training: key to institutional improvement, *Readings in the Administration of Institutions for Delinquent Youth.* Springfield, Thomas, p. 42, 1965.

INDEX

193